My 38 Years in the Chain Gang

by

Cliff Gilley

authorHOUSE™

1663 LIBERTY DRIVE, SUITE 200
BLOOMINGTON, INDIANA 47403
(800) 839-8640
WWW.AUTHORHOUSE.COM

First published by AuthorHouse 08/16/04

ISBN: 1-4184-9540-9 (e)
ISBN: 1-4184-9541-7 (sc)

Printed in the United States of America
Bloomington, Indiana

This book is printed on acid-free paper.

This book is dedicated to my lovely daughter, Melinda Gilley Cort, for her tireless effort of entering this book into her computer, making publication possible.

TABLE OF CONTENTS

PREFACE

It is the general concept of the adult population of the world that when they hear of a book about the "Chain Gang", it must consist from cover to cover of brutality, degradation, inhumane, bloody fighting and any other demon-possessed action known to man. Not so in this book entitled, "My 38 Years in the Chain Gang." It consists of a sprinkling of misconduct and insubordination, but you will find it bearable and many times "humorous"!! The author's intention was not to horrify the reader nor billify the officers and instructors of this first offender, minimum security institution, but to bring the reader a pleasant, enjoyable few hours of entertainment and information about the concealed lifestyle of the inmates and staff.

CHAPTER 1
LEARNING THE ROPES

Sometimes I wonder about the circumstances we find ourselves in. That is the case of my 38 years in the chain gang. This is how it started. In 1948, when I graduated from high school in Lynch, Kentucky, I made up my mind that I wanted to be a railroad office worker. I applied, and was received in Chillicothee Business School. I completed the school with a certificate which said I could telegraph 25 words per minute.

I came to Montgomery, Alabama in March, 1949, and was hired as a clerk telegraph agent with the A.C.L.R.R. (Atlantic Coast Line Rail Road). I worked in the Montgomery area for two years until I was drafted into Military service. In February 1954, I finished my tour of duty, but when I called the A.C.L.R.R., they told me that I had been rolled off my job in Montgomery. The only regular job I could hold with my seniority was a 4 to 12 pm operator's job at the Chattahoochee, Florida A.C.L.R.R. office. I worked there until March 1st, 1958.

In the meantime, I had met the superintendent, and the business manager from Apalachee Correctional Institution (ACI) in Sneads, Florida. I told them that I had been rolled again and they said, "Why don't you come over and work for us?" Well, as soon as my displacement was official, I went to the superintendent's office and said, "Here I am. I decided to take you up on that job offer." The next day the superintendent called in the business manager, and said to him, "Mr. Gilley has decided to take us up on our job offer. What do you have for him?" The business manager replied, "Much to my dismay, nothing right now, but let me see what I can do, and I will let him know." The next day the business manager came to my house, and told me that the only thing he had to offer was a truck driving job that paid only $240 a month, which was exactly half of my income with the railroad. He suggested, however, that I take it to get my foot in the door, because the institution was only nine years old, and growing by leaps and bounds. I accepted his offer, and started the first day of my long 38 year career.

When I reported for work, I was told I had to go through a one-week orientation. The personnel manager told me I was lucky that I would not have to go through orientation alone. There were two other new employees, and all three of us would go through it together. Now, these three new employees were a strange contrast. One was a Baptist ordained preacher, who was the first chaplain that ACI ever had; the second was a Methodist preacher, who had been hired to be the assistant coach, and myself the ex-railroad telegrapher destined to start as a delivery truck driver.

Everything went well with the orientation until the fifth day, but then the train derailed! That day we were supposed to be oriented to the security department by the chief custodial officer, but he had an emergency, so we were held over in the waiting room of the administration building. There sat the three of us on a couch, me in the middle, with a preacher on either side, when the door burst open, and an employee of the Florida State Hospital (a nearby mental institution) came rushing in. He exclaimed, "We were coming west on Highway 90" (the road in front of ACI) "when your blue and white 2-ton delivery truck pulled up and stopped at the highway. As soon as the truck stopped, one of the inmates in the middle of the seat grabbed the driver around the neck and started hitting him in the head. The inmate on the outside ran around to the other side of the truck, jerked the driver's door open, shoved the driver over to the middle of the seat and drove the truck away. We rushed straight here to report it." he was so excited and talking so loudly, that the lieutenant, the superintendent, the captain, plus several others had gathered in the lobby where we were now all standing.

At this time, things started to pop. The lieutenant, who was an old retired first sergeant from World War II ran out in the middle of the floor, looked at the three of us in orientation. He knew each of our backgrounds. It didn't take him long to decide he would rather have an ex-railroad man than a preacher to go with him chasing escaped convicts.

I ran out behind the lieutenant. He jumped under the steering wheel of a pickup truck, and yelled, "Get in!" I did, and we scratched off. I had no idea where we were going. As we left the exterior fence, we flew on two wheels most of the way to the dog yard. When we got there, the sergeant was ready with two bloodhounds, and two inmate trustees who were used as dog handlers. The sergeant jumped into the front seat with the lieutenant and me. As I looked back through the rear window, I saw the two dogs and their handlers make one lurch and all four were in the truck bed lying down.

The sergeant reached over in front of me and turned on the two-way radio. He said "That truck has a radio in it, and they probably have it on. I want them to know we are after them. They will know the chase pickups are much faster than that big old delivery truck, and maybe they will abandon it before they get too far away." I said, "Makes sense."

The lieutenant said, "Whatever the sergeant says makes sense. He's been chasing runaways hundreds of times." We headed west on 90 wide open. Being in the middle of the seat in a chase pickup leaves very little to hold on to, so I just hunkered up, and bounced around.

I asked the lieutenant where we were going, and he said he didn't know. Just as we were leaving Sneads, someone came on the radio. It was the driver of the delivery truck that had been kidnapped. The Sgt. grabbed the radio and said into it, "Where are you man?" The voice on the radio came back, "Four miles north of Four Points."

We liked to have lost it when the lieutenant slammed on the brakes, and turned sideways just at the right time to slide onto a dirt road heading north. No one said anything. I think we were too scared. I looked at the lieutenant. He was just watching the road ahead. If anyone is not familiar with a country dirt road that is well-traveled, let me tell you, the road becomes like a washboard. You try to go fast on a road like that, and it is murder!! All this time, the captured officer was talking to the control room on the radio, but we couldn't make out what he was saying because of all the rattling of the old pickup, and the dogs barking. I think they were scared to death too.

As we rounded a curve, there was the big blue and white delivery truck. The captured officer was standing there in a pair of pants three sizes too big, with only a tee shirt on, and it was covered in blood. The Sgt. jumped out with the two dogs and handlers. The truck driver pointed to the east and said, "Both of them went that way." That whole bunch, 2 dogs, 2 handlers, and the Sgt. hadn't gone a hundred yards before the Sgt. yelled, "Here is one!" I'm cuffing him to a tree. Come get him! I'm going after the other one!" The lieutenant started across the field and then asked the Sgt. if he needed me. He said, "No, you see what you can do for the truck driver." I checked the truck driver to see where the blood had come from, and found he had a gash in his head. The bleeding had clotted though, and stopped flowing. From my orientation, I knew we had a medical department at the institution, and thought it would be best to get him back to them.

Just about this time, only a few minutes since we arrived at the scene, around the corner came the superintendent in an old blue and white station wagon. He must have been traveling 75 miles per hour, and by the time he saw us, he couldn't stop. He passed us by, and traveled at least 50 yards down the road. As soon as he stopped moving, he put it in reverse, and as he came backwards, (He wasn't too good at driving backwards...or forwards either for that matter) he ran into the ditch on the right side of the road once, and the ditch on the left side of the road twice. He was going so fast, he went into those ditches and right back out again. Finally, he got stopped right in front of the truck.

I had not asked the driver any of the details because I knew he would have to tell it all over again when the superintendent got there. It had not entered my mind that I was supposed to be driving that same delivery truck today, and had <u>NOT</u> driven because I was waiting for security orientation. When the supt. got to us, the first thing he said to me was, "Mr. Gilley, what do you think about this now?" I said, "Mr. superintendent, I ain't worried about this. It probably won't happen again for two or three weeks!"

I thought the driver was being very cool and brave about the whole thing, but when the supt. asked what happened, he lost it. He broke down and cried like a baby. He was scared breathless. This had been a dangerous situation. Those inmates could have killed this man. When he regained his composure, the truck driver told us that the big inmate took the truck driver's clothes, put them on, and locked the driver in the back of the truck. The inmate's pants had a pair of nail nippers in them. The driver took the nail nippers and cut the cotter key which held the pin in the top and bottom latches in place. When he got the cotter key out, the pin could be pushed out and the latches fell free. Then he went around to the radio and called in. He was grateful that they had not thought to destroy the radio.

By this time, the Sgt. was back with the first captured inmate. The supt. said, "Leave him handcuffed behind his back, and put him in the station wagon." As soon as the door slammed on the first capture, we heard a noise from the weed patch, and here came the Sgt. with the other escapee. I thought, "Boy, there ain't nothing to catching escaped inmates."

I heard many tales about that escape later. Some said they weren't trying to get away, they just wanted to get even with the truck driver. No matter the reason, it really messed up the driver. Four weeks later, when he returned to work, he could not make himself come back inside that fence. God bless the truck driver!

The reason for the inmates' actions were merely speculation, but all the rest of this story is absolutely true. I've been there and done that!!

CHAPTER 2
CI HISTORY

Now that you've read about my first weeks at Apalachee Correctional Institution (ACI), I need to tell you about ACI. ACI was opened in 1949 as a minimum security youthful offenders, ages 14-24 institution. It was designed for 250 inmates. It was fully independent with it's own electrical plant, it's own sewage disposal plant, and also, it's own steam boiler plant using coal for fuel. The coal was delivered to Chattahoochee, Florida on railroad cars and had to be trucked to ACI across the Apalachicola River by ACI employees.

I worked my way up through the ranks from truck driver to stock clerk, the accountant clerk, to equipment custodian, and then, in 13 years to purchasing agent. I decided that was it for me, so I turned down promotions that were offered from the state office in Tallahassee, and Marianna after that. I remained as purchasing agent at ACI for 25 years. The institution's top staff were: superintendent, assistant superintendent, business manager and the purchasing agent. These were, in my opinion, just the four jobs needed to run the institution effectively. But the top four jobs have now been abolished. Governor Bush hired himself a

7

hatchet man from Texas, and now all the institutions in the State of Florida are just holding pens.

Now there is nothing for the inmates to do, or learn. They just sit on their bunks and watch TV. In 1958, when I was hired by ACI, every one of the inmates that were not on sick call, had a job to do, or a school class to attend. Every man that did not have a high school diploma went to school half time...2 days a week, 3 days the next week, until he received his diploma, went home on parole, or was declared by the school psychiatrists to be incapable of learning.

There were only 7 prisons in the State of Florida in 1958, and the 7th one was ACI. There were 450 inmates and 150 officers at that time. We had already outgrown the electric plant and were hooked up to an outside power plant (Gulf Power). We had also outgrown our sewage plant, and had to be hooked up to the city of Sneads for that.

ACI was the pride of the Department of Corrections at that time. The education department at ACI was issuing 150 high school diplomas every year. They had 13 well-educated teachers on staff, and a complex second to none. The county schools were jealous of our science lab. It was equal to Florida State University's I was told.

When I retired in 1995, there were 2000 inmates, and 500 officers, and 4 industries at ACI. Over 15 years' time there had been 17 different industries for the inmates to work in there. The department heads in Tallahassee got tired of the worries over the industries, and got the legislature to privatize the industries program. They turned it over to PRIDE. Now, at ACI there are only 2 industries left. The rest have gone out the window, with no return. Along with them, the wonderful job learning opportunities.

Well, now that you know about ACI, let me get on with my story. True story that is. On my first day of truck driving, my headquarters was the warehouse. I picked up my two inmates there, and returned them at the same place by 12 noon for lunch. The state fed all employees for free at that time. It was the same food that the inmates ate...nothing to write home about, but it was nourishing and healthy.

I picked up my two inmates that first day, and there was a note on my food to deliver a shipment to the construction site where our staff was building a new dorm. They had constructed a temporary warehouse on the site. I knew where it was because of orientation. I wheeled in between the two new dorms and up on top of the hill to the construction warehouse. Just as I turned that big old van type truck in front of the warehouses, I heard a loud bong like I had hit something, or something had hit me. I stopped, and sure enough, I heard someone yelling at the top of their voice, "You idiot! Can't you see you've run into our phone line?" They had recently put a phone line out to the warehouse, and the top of my van had caught the low slung line which had been propped up by a single 2 X 4. I jumped out of my truck, and yelled back at the man, "Who put that rat trap up?" The big tough guy said, "Not me, the telephone man." As I pulled the broken phone line off of my cab, I said to the big tough guy (who, by the way, was the electrician, and later became one of my favorite people), "Tell that telephone man we are going to have a drove of semis coming in here, and he better get a longer clothes line pole." I never heard any more about this incident.

In 1960, a young man came to work in our business office as an accountant. He was from Bracken County, Kentucky. We became great friends, being from the same home state, Kentucky. My heart is heavy as I was told Sunday that he died in his sleep the night before. He and I worked at ACI for 30 years together. He was the business manager for 20 years, and that meant he was my boss. I must tell you a funny story about us both being from Kentucky. One day during our office Christmas party, one of the seven ladies working in the business office asked me about where we both came from. I told them I was from the mountains where we made moonshine and I was hauling into Tennessee, and the business manager (Charlie) was working for the Revenue Department of KY. One girl said, "Yes, I saw his resume. He did work for that department." I said, "Well, one day I decided to leave and get out of the moonshine business, but Charlie wouldn't give up. He trailed me to ACI and told me that my time was up. I had to go back. I told him, 'Well, OK, but first I want to take you fishing.' We went and caught our limit plus some. He told me that he sure did hate to leave this place. I said, 'Just wait until hunting season. I told him, 'I'll get you a job at ACI if you don't take me back.'" Of course, that was not true, but someone called on me to return thanks at that time, and I never did remember to tell those ladies that I was just teasing. Later I was told the ladies knew I was just teasing. That made me feel better.

Now, back to my truck driving. The rest of my first day, I just made little short trips to the auto shop for parts. The second day was the day to deliver fresh fryers to the Florida State Hospital. We had a slaughter house at poultry where the people killed and dressed frying sized chickens. We purchased them one day old for 2-1/2 cents each, 3,500 at a time and furnished them dressed at 4 months old. This morning, when I backed my truck up to that slaughter house door and when in, I thought, "Oh my Lord, what have I gotten myself into?" The poultry supervisor saw me and grinned from ear to ear. He was 6'5" tall, with hands like sides of pork. He shook hands with me and said, "I heard you were taking the job Mr. Gilley, and I am sure you will do a good job." They were not quite finished, so I watched the operation. There was a long metal tunnel with water running down the walls and bottom of the floor to carry the blood away. The operator had on extra thick blood gloves to match his heavy black apron. They were sorting the chickens, putting 6 per rack and the racks were on wheels on the trolley. The inmate at the tunnel entrance would reach out and get a chicken by the head and cut it's throat with the electric knife. The chicken would not flop or make a sound. After he had killed all six, he pushed the rack of chickens into the tunnel. That rack pushed through the one ahead of it. There was a kettle of boiling water at the end of the tunnel and a man would dump the chickens into a vat. There were two men with long rubber gloves taking the chickens out of the vat, holding them by the feet, and putting them on the picker which was a 48" diameter drum with hundreds of rubber fingers. These fingers which were about six inches long, had rings around on them, and made the feathers fly. As soon as they were defeathered, they were thrown upon a long stainless steel table. There was the starting of the dressing table. When they reached the end of that table, the chickens were ready for the trip. Into the can they would go. When the can was full, they put ice on it and then my men would take the can and put it on my truck. The poultry supervisor said, "Stick around as long as you can, Mr. Gilley." I said, "I've had enough of this stink and noise!"

There were 7 kitchens at the Florida State Hospital to feed 8,000 mental patients and 4,000 employees. I had to haul all the chickens and eggs that would feed and fill that many people.

When we got to the general kitchen, we found it was the largest kitchen of all. I parked at the unloading ramp and told my two inmates to come with me to get a 4 wheel truck to unload the cans onto. The three of us started down the long hallway to the general kitchen office. About halfway down the hall, in front of the coolers, we met a huge black man weighing about 250 pounds. He was shadow boxing. He had his chin down on his massive chest and was jabbing with his left fist while he protected his face with his right fist. He was snorting like a professional boxer as he came toward me. I called on my knowledge of the Florida State Mental Institution and remembered that they had a Forensic unit which housed violent patients. Then I resorted to self-preservation reasoning and thought to myself, "I have a big heavy metal clip board in my right hand," I reasoned "that big black dude has one punch coming, and if he throws it at me or my men, I will fram him up side his big ugly head, and knock him into the middle of next week." Just at that moment, I heard a voice in my ear saying, "You want me to take him, Mr. Gilley?" It was one of my inmates coming to my aid. I said, "No thanks, I'll handle it." The big dude just went right on by us dancing, snorting and punching the air till he reached the end of the hall. Then he turned around and came back doing the same thing. The inmate with me said, "That guy is crazy." I replied, "You hit the nail on the head son!" I told the cook in the office what had happened in the hall. He laughed and said, "Yeah, that's Irvin. He's been doing that ever since he saw Joe Lewis on TV." I said, "Has anyone ever hit him?" The guy said, "I don't think so, but he has scared off several salesmen, so I just let him have his fun."

I worked out of the warehouse and business office. They had from 15 to 20 inmates assigned to them. They let me pick who I wanted to go with me to do the labor of pickup and delivering. I looked over the crew to see who I liked the looks of, to be with me outside the fence. I liked this man who offered to take that pretend boxer. I checked his record to see what he was pulling time for. I found out that he and his girlfriend had taken her father's yacht out on the Gulf at Panama City and spent the day. When they started back in, the yacht had lost all it's power. No lights, no radio, no nothing. They were out three days before the Coast Guard found them. The girl's father threw the book at him. Luckily the girl was of age, but they got him for theft. I decided I could stand that. He was 20 years old and 5'10" tall, weighed 180 pounds with a good build. He could handle the cans and cases real easy, so I talked to him about being a regular on my truck. He was tickled to be able to go outside the compound.

I found another good sized man who was in for breaking and entering. I got the two of them together out by the truck and told them my rules and regulations. I said, "They are simple: no waving or calling out to the people we pass; if a person speaks, be polite and answer questions, but do not offer any information. I only have two instructions: number one is, I'm always boss; number two is, if any doubt arises, refer to rule number one!" Sometimes, I had to use another inmate, but when available, I took these two. I worked the truck for nine months, and never had a moment's trouble out of the men.

I picked up bread two times a week, 200 loaves each time in big metal boxes with attached lids, which totaled 400 loaves a week. The bread was still warm when we picked it up. It smelled delicious. One day one of my men asked me if they could have a loaf to eat. I said, "Yes, one loaf, but don't take any back to the institution." That was the policy I always followed when I gave them anything.

We had to have fresh milk from the FSU dairy which was 15 milk cans full twice a week. They made chocolate milk in 1/2 pint jars. The man in charge of the dairy would give me a carton of twelve for me and my men. I would drink two and let the men drink the other 10 if they could. They would drink them all before they got back to the compound.

I must tell you about what happened at the bakery one day. The man in charge of the bakery had about 5 mental patients working in the bakery. The patients were real friendly and while my men were loading the loaves of bread, the patients would come over and talk with me. There was one big man who spoke with a lisp, and his left arm was permanently bent and frozen at the elbow. I asked him why his arm was like that. He said that when he was a child, he fell and broke his arm. His mother put it in a sling and left it there for two years. One day I asked that patient why he was in a mental institution, because he seemed plenty capable of living outside. He told me this story: He pointed to another patient and said, "That is my brother. Me and him was robbing a service station. He was inside getting the money and stuff and left me outside to watch for the cops. Well, the police came around and caught both of us." Then the patient said to me in all sincerity, "My brother said to me, 'I told you to watch for the police.' I said I did watch for them, and I saw them. Then my brother said, 'Why didn't you tell me they were here?' Then I told him, you didn't say a thing about telling you when they came, you just told me to watch for them and I did." Then he told me that when this all came out at trial, the judge said he had the very place for both of us, and here we are. Then he slapped me on the shoulder, let out a big snort, and away he went. I looked around and there was the supervisor. I shrugged my shoulders and flung my hands out. The supervisor said, "It was all true."

One day I was on the hospital grounds and had stopped, parked, my big old truck, and told the helpers to wait for me. I would be right back. Just as I slid out of the cab, there was a little bitty man about 5 feet tall and he walked right up to me and said, "Give me a nickel." I felt sorry for him and I felt in my pocket for some change, only to remember I had left it on the dresser that morning. So, I took a dollar bill out of my wallet, handed it to him and said, "I don't have a nickel. Will this do?" "Yes," he said, and as I turned to leave, he said, "Wait a minute." He ran his hand down into his front pocket to his elbow and pulled out an old dirty sock. It was attached to the bottom of his pocket with a big safety pin. He unpinned it and detached the sock from his pocket. It was not accessible, though because it was tied in a hard knot. When he finally got his hand into the sock, I could tell it was filled with something. I didn't know what, but to my amazement, it was full of money. He rammed his hand down to the bottom past a large amount of bills of all sizes, brought out a hand full of change, and gave me 95 cents. He then thanked me, and proceeded to reverse the procedure of tying a knot in the sock, pinning it to the bottom of his pocket, stuffing it way down in his pocket, and started off looking for another client. When I got into the accounting office, I said, "You won't believe what just happened to me." They said, "You had to donate a nickel, and got 95 cents in change." I said, "How did you know that?" They said, "We saw you through the window. Sometimes he has hundreds of dollars in that old dirty sock." I said, "From now on, I'm going to be sure to have a nickel in my pocket."

One day when I was delivering eggs to the hospital, I went into the poultry office to pickup my shipping documents and there on the supervisor's desk were two eggs. I burst out in a healthy belly laugh. The officer asked what was so funny. I pointed at the eggs. One was as big as a baseball, and the other one was the size of a bird's egg. I picked the big one up and said, "What do you call this one?" He said, "Extra large jumbo, and the small one is called extra small pee wee." I said, "I bet the hen that laid this big one must have been in pain." He said, "It caused what we call a blow-out, and we had to destroy the hen." "What about this one?" I

14

asked holding up the pee wee. He said, "That is just the first egg that a hen ever laid. That's normal." I said, "Can I have these eggs? I'll have some fun when I deliver the eggs today." "Sure," he said, "I don't want them."

As I remember this day, it was cold weather in late October because I had on my college football jacket. I put one egg in one pocket and one in the other pocket. I went to the egg house and picked up a load of eggs. We shipped the eggs in galvanized sheet metal crates that would hold 30 dozen each. They were pretty strong and you could stack them pretty high, but they were not very steady when you stacked them more than four high. On this day, I delivered the small kitchens first and had a ball with the cooks, offering them a real good price on my eggs today, if they would accept shipment of these eggs and showing them Mr. pee wee. Most every one refused to accept the pee wee. But, they did all laugh. Then they really laughed when I offered them the baseball sized one! When we got to the general kitchen, they had several cases of eggs left over from the last shipment. My inmates had to stack the eggs over five cases high to get them all in the cooler. Just as they finished stacking the eggs and were leaving the cooler, I looked back at the stack of cases, and they were starting to lean toward me. I yelled and ran to the stack of eggs. I threw myself belly first against the eggs to keep them from falling, and yelled for my men to start unstacking the cases. Luckily none fell, and we told the supervisor that we could either stack the cases on the floor, or in another cooler, but that I wouldn't have my men stack them so high again, because we almost had a wreck. The cook said we could just set them on the floor. I looked at one of my helpers. He was looking at me with a sly grin on his face, and I said, "What?" Then, it struck me like a ton of bricks....I ran my hand in my jacket pockets, and boy oh boy!!! Both of the eggs had broken. One pocket was not so bad, but the other one was full of jumbo fresh raw egg!! Both the inmates were trying to keep from laughing. I said, "Get outside, and laugh all you want to, but don't let me hear you!"

Amos Infirmary was the smallest kitchen where we made deliveries. One day, I was delivering three cans of fresh iced-down broilers, and as I came into the drive, I noticed that there was an auto parked at the unloading ramp. There was a ramp built way out on the side of the driveway going to the halls. Rather than go try to find the owner and get them to move their car, I backed across the driveway just in front of the car and went inside to unload the three cans. I wasn't in the kitchen more than five minutes, but when I came out there was a 6'5" jackass blowing his top because he was blocked in. When he saw me going to get in the truck, he said, "Where in the hell did you learn to drive?" I replied, "The same place you learned to park and block loading docks!" The cook was standing on the dock listening to all that was said. The next day, the cook said, "You must not know who you were talking to yesterday." "I don't care who he was" The cook said, "That man was Dr. Bimbo, the chief surgeon of the whole hospital." I said, "Like I said, I don't care who he is. He doesn't sign my pay check, and I'll bet he doesn't block any more unloading docks."

Along with everything else that I hauled from Florida State Hospital, I hauled all of the vegetables from their general kitchen. Twice a week I would haul 10 blocks of ice which were 300 pounds each. I don't remember ever having anything interesting to happen to me while on a vegetable or ice run.

One thing that I look back on with great delight is the friends that I met while shopping around Tallahassee, when I went over to pickup milk. I remember IF & WB Drew Office Supply Co. That lady would send her office boy around to other stores and pickup items for me because you can't park that big old truck just anywhere. In the same story ACI had an employees softball team. There were only four teams on the league: two from the hospital, one from the city and one from ACI. I lived in the city, but I played with ACI. We played two nights a week. One night I was contacted by one of the hospital's manager's who told me that the Tallahassee softball league had offered us a chance to play in a tournament which would be held in Tallahassee beginning the next night. He told me they had offered for us to take the best of all four teams and come over to play in the place vacated by Mobile, AL. We managed to get ten men willing to go. We were to play the bankers' team. They were the prettiest team I have ever seen. Their uniforms were bright red and white. Their shoes were all shined to perfection. Their black belts were too. They looked like they had just stepped out of a fashion magazine. When they were getting their infield practice, our men were all sitting on the bench. I said to them, "You guys want to go home?" Our big old catcher who played barefoot, with his pants legs rolled up to his knees said, "Looks ain't never won nothing but a fashion show. That ain't what this is, is it?" "Looks like it might be," someone said.

When it came time for ACI's team to get infield practice, I looked around at the players, and could not keep from laughing. We had no caps, no uniforms, old ragged clothes including tank top shirts. To make a long story short, we beat those pretty boys 2-0. I have to give the credit to our pitcher who was the head coach at ACI. With long hairy arms, he could fling that fast pitch softball better than anyone else I ever saw. He only gave up one hit in the game. Needless to say, there was a deafening silence over the crowd in the full stands that night after the game. All the spectators were there for the bankers, and not a single person came to cheer for us. We were scheduled to play a second game the next morning which was Saturday and back in those days we were working 5 1/2 days a week....including Saturday morning until noon. Only four of our team could go, so we had to forfeit the second game. But, we made our statement in the first game and had our fun!

I only drove that old truck for nine months, but it seemed like years. I still, 40 years later, have nightmares about driving over that old narrow bridge across the Apalachicola River. It was high, and my truck was so high, that I could look down from the cab and see over the guard rail right into that old muddy river. That wasn't even the bad part. The bridge was so narrow you could hardly pass any oncoming traffic. I hit the bridge guard rail twice in that period of time, and two semi-trucks hit my rear view mirrors.

They were building a new bridge over the river and it was a big wide pretty thing. The strangest thing was, though, the next day after they opened it, I was transferred into the office of my new job, and off of the truck. I never got to drive on the new bridge with that truck.

CHAPTER 3
FROM TRUCKING TO POSTING

On the first of November, I was transferred into the office to an accountant clerk's job. The business office was in one corner of the warehouse that had been walled-in and housed 5 officers and 15 inmates. The inmates were used to type everything, such as inventory lists, receiving registers, purchase orders, even payment vouchers. My first and main job was to supervise the inmate that was doing invoice vouchers. I told the inmate to show me everything that was involved in scheduling invoices. I said to myself and the other officers, I was not going to supervise a worker unless I could do their job myself. I did that for 36 years. I guess that is why I never got any higher than purchasing agent. But, that was high enough for me, and I loved it.

My first assignment on the new job was to get everything ready to make Christmas packages for all 450 of the inmates. I made a list of what I wanted for the Christmas bags, and, that is just what they were...number 12 brown paper bags. I planned to give them one apple, one orange, one pound of mixed nuts, one pound of hard candy, and two packs of cigarettes. Yes, cigarettes. The state furnished smoking tobacco with roll-your-own papers. So, I gave them two packs of Pall Mall ready rolls. I turned my want list over to the business manager, and he turned it over to the purchasing agent, and by the 18th of December, it was all in the warehouse. I asked for permission to close down work in the office so I could use all the inmates to stuff the bags. Permission granted, I went to the construction department, got a sheet of 4'X 8' plywood, and nailed a 2 X 4 across each end, and one down the sides. That was to keep anything from rolling off. I got two saw horses, turned the plywood with the 2 X 4 sides up, and put the saw horses in the middle of the office with plywood on top. We started stuffing the bags. I lined the inmates up around the table and each one had a job to do. One man put in the apple, one the orange, and so on around the table. The candy (which included orange slices and chocolate drops) came packaged in 15 pound boxes, which had to be bagged in small bags. I told the inmates they could eat all they wanted, but could not carry any of the treats out of the office. The Purchasing Agent said, "Man you should know what you just said. They will eat it all up." "No, they won't," I said. Sure enough they had their fill in short order. I sent inmates to the laundry just across the street to get 6 laundry carts to put the bags in when completed. We fixed 12 extra bags, because I knew some would be lost. Christmas eve, we left the laundry carts in line in the middle of the floor with instructions for the on-duty correctional officers to bring inmates into our office, and get the gifts for distribution to the inmates on Christmas morning. Those of us in the warehouse and office had more important things to do at home than to hand out Christmas gifts. I was surprised how well the project went.

I was in the process of making a set of control cards for the warehouse inventory cost control. I was knee-deep in work at my new desk a week later, when the Purchasing Agent, who was also the office manager, dropped a set of keys on my desk and said, "They need you to drive a coal truck today." The boilers that made steam for the kitchen, and heat for the dormitories used coal for fuel. There was a train car load at the Florida State Hospital rail siding waiting on us to come get it. The discipline squad had already gone over with their boss to start shoveling coal as soon as we arrived. There were three trucks running coal, and we would run to the institution and dump a load, while the squad would be loading the next truck. I had made three trips, and was coming down the hill to the river bridge when the hood of the old truck I was driving flew up, and went right back over the cab. I stuck my head out the window, which was minus a glass, so I could see how to stop. Once I got stopped, I looked under the seat and found a piece of wire, and wired it down, so I could keep on trucking.

If you have never visited a minimum security prison, it's hard to believe how lax the staff there is. It is run like an honor system. At A.C.I. in the 1950's and up through the 90's, there were only 2 ways in and out of the prison, east gate and west gate which were both double gates swinging over the road. The gate at east end was opened in the morning, and remained open until 5 pm when the work crews of inmates came back from their daily work. The officers and inmates just came and went as they pleased. Each officer that had a crew was instructed to count his men once every hour to be sure that no one left. Sometimes when you have a bunch of inmates scattered all over creation, it's almost impossible to keep check on them until lunch time, or quitting time. In orientation, the inmates are told that if they want to escape and run away, to go ahead, but we have 40 or more bloodhounds, and if you leave, we'll come and get you. At the time, 40 inmates had run, and every one had been caught. There were only 2 that had gotten all the way to Australia on a ship, stayed two years, but didn't like it, so they came back to California. They were picked up in two weeks and we went out to California and brought them back. Anytime an inmate got away, he was put on all points bulletin all over the USA All law enforcement officers were on the lookout for them. But there was always someone who got what we called the "Rabbit Fever" : Then we all would get on the trail, and sooner or later, we would get him.

One day while business was as usual, I was at my desk when they called me to come go on a chase. One had left from the saw mill. I was given a Truck, a gun, and told to go up to Back Country, Georgia to catch the escapee. I had on a gray suit coat and white shirt with a blue straw hat. I put the pistol and holster on my belt on the right side and put the tail of my coat behind the gun, put the brim of my hat down all the way around . Now I thought, "I'm ready". I looked in every culvert, every bush, and knocked on every door, and told whoever answered the door that I was an investigator, and asked if they had seen a man in blue clothes with a white stripe down the leg. They naturally told me they hadn't seen one. So I spent half a day looking, and had decided to work my way back South toward the saw mill. As I rounded a curve, there sat two State pickup trucks. They were pulled up nose to nose. On one pickup was the captain from the West Unit, on the other hood was the Supervisor of the Brick Plant. I wheeled up to them, got out and said, "I thought we were on a chase." The captain replied, "Take it easy, son. He'll show up when it gets lunch time." Right at that minute a message came in on all three of our radios: "Attention all units, the Signal 6 is off. The suspect has shown up in the chow line at the West Unit." I asked the captain how he knew that. He said that he would come back at lunch time. He also said, "The inmate has a girlfriend in the woods up there, and slips off to see her real often, but we haven't been able to catch him." I said, "Well, I have been on my first snipe hunt."

My job description reads to maintain cost accounting cards, keep account of inmates in my charge, but the last statement was the killer, and any related duties necessary to keep the institution running; when a rail car of coal was received at the hospital, they first called the business office to get drivers for the coal pickup. There were only four of us in the office and usually two of us younger ones would go and haul coal. At first, the discipline squad would go over with shovels and unload the cars. Later on, the institution got an old dragline from somewhere and it had a clamshell bucket. There was one inmate who knew how to operate it. He was the oldest inmate at A.C.I. age 29. If the inmate reached 24, (which was the age limit), with a good record, and was working an important job, he would be left until the end of his sentence, or his parole. Finally this man was offered a job in New Jersey making more money than the superintendent at ACI. He would be a heavy equipment operator. He was certainly good on that old dragline. He could thread a needle with that thing. I know, the first time I saw him operating that clamshell under the high voltage lines over the coal cars, I kept my distance. Finally I realized he was not going to get into those lines. Then I didn't even think about it any more. When this inmate left, someone came up with the idea of having the coal car delivered to the spur track. They took a bulldozer and dug a passage under the track so we could back a truck down the ramp under the rail. There was a chute for dumping the coal out into the truck. Once the truck had a load, there was a shut off lever to keep the coal from falling out of the car. It worked fine for years. One day I had hauled one load, and when I went back, the whole pit under the car was full of coal, and all the people were gathered at the side of the ramp. I backed down to the pile of coal, and stopped. I got out and went over where the crowd was. It was only then that I saw an inmate sitting on a 5 gallon bucket with coal dust all over him. He had it in his hair, ears, eyes, and pockets full too. I asked, "What happened?" I was told that the coal had been in rain and cold weather on it's way to us. When we unloaded a truck load out of the car, it bridged over and would not come out. The two inmates on top of the car tried to get the bridge-over to break, and let more coal come out. But, they could not get the coal started with their shovels. One of the men jumped onto the bridge of coal, and when he did, the bridge-over broke loose. The inmate fell into the coal, with the sides of the coal falling in on top of him, covering him completely. The coal was ground up to be used in a stoker-fed furnace. The grains of coal were the size of peas. Luckily it wasn't ground into a powder. The second inmate jumped into the coal and put his hand over the trapped man's face to keep the coal from smothering him. All the while yelling for someone to open the chute door. The officer managing the brick plant ran into the pit and pulled the lever, releasing the coal. This brought the trapped inmate into the pit, and the other inmate managed to scramble up the side of the loose coal and grab hold of the side and top of the car, and climb out. Neither of the inmates were any worse than scared breathless. The brick plant loaned us some shovels and some inmates to load the dumped coal from the ground. We were only delayed about an hour of time, and the two inmates probably scared out of ten years' growth. Just another day in the chain gang.

I always wanted to be involved in everything going.

Our population of inmates was increasing by leaps and bounds. The institution ordered a new machine for the laundry, a commercial type washer. It weighed 8,200 pounds, and was built like a square box about 8 feet long, 6 feet high and 6 feet wide. It came to us by semi-truck. The purchasing agent came to me for my opinion on how to get it off the truck. I asked, "You want me to handle it for your bosses?" He doubtingly asked, "Can you do it?" I had never done such a thing, but I knew how to do it. I went out back, got the four biggest inmates available, and told the delivery man to move down away from the door to a less-used part of the dock. I went to the tool rack, got two five-foot pry bars, three six-foot lengths of 2 inch steel pipes, and started to work. I told my helpers not to get in a hurry, and don't get a finger caught. First we put one pipe down for a lever, and two men on pinch bars, lifted the end of the machine far enough to get a piece of pipe under the bottom front of the load. That done, we went to the rear, and pinched the load forward onto the pipe. It only moved about two inches. "Good job," I declared. One of the inmates said, "Sir?" I said, "A trip of a mile begins with two inches." As the load moved to the rear of the truck, we would slip another pipe under it. We soon had the machine riding on pipes. All we had to do was pinch it along. When we got to the back of the truck, the machine was about four inches higher than the loading dock. I told the men just to let it down easy with the pinch bars. It only took about 25 minutes to get the machine unloaded. The delivery man said, "I thought it would take at least half a day." I said, "I'm sorry. I thought you were in a hurry." He said, "No, I get paid by the hour." "Well," I said, "You can't please everyone. "

When they got ready to install the new laundry machine, the purchasing agent came back to me while I was working on inventory cards, and asked real sweetly if I could get that machine down from the ramp and across to the laundry. I was already suspicious that they would ask me to move it. So, I got out into the construction site, and found some huge timbers and railroad cross ties. I got a truck and went to the site. I asked the construction supervisor if I could borrow some timbers to move that machine to the laundry. "How do you propose to do that?" "It's so complicated to explain, you wouldn't understand" I said, "and they are waiting on me to get back.'" I placed the cross ties across, laid the big 4 inch thick timbers length ways of the proposed ramp and started pinching this machine down the ramp, letting the rear drag all the way to keep it from running away once we got started down the ramp. To make a long story short, I put the machine in the laundry by pure man-power, or I might say, boy power. None of the four inmates I used were as old as 20 years. From that day until the day the laundry supervisor, and the purchasing agent retired, both were as good a friend as I ever had.

When I first hired out, the institution had a little bitty house in which the soap factory operated, mixing chemicals to a perfected formula and peddled it to other state institutions. We manufactured about 25 kinds of soap including, laundry, kitchen, and personal hygiene soaps. The little building was too small, so we used part of our warehouse to store raw materials and also finished products. All these were in the bulk fiber drums which held 75 pounds to 125 pounds capacity. When a truck load of chemicals came in, we would take all of the office men out to the warehouse to help unload the truck. I would help supervise. We had two inmates that were handicapped. The oldest of this pair was 23 years old, married and had one child. In the summer of 1959, he received a letter from his wife that informed him that she had a new baby. Oh joy!! The bad thing about this situation was that the inmate had been locked up for 2-1/2 years. This man did not have any faith in our counselor, but he had worked for me for 6 months, so he decided to trust in me. He talked with me and even asked me what he should do. I took him out on the far end of the dock where no one could hear us. When we were sure no one was hearing, I told him: "Do not let the other inmates know this. They will just goad you into running away, and going home to beat her to a pulp, and kill the other man. Next, all I can tell you, it's up to you. You'll have to decide whether or not you are going to forgive your wife, and accept that child as your own. Or you can divorce her and go on without her. But, don't be hasty. Live with it for several days. Think about it at night, and during broad daylight." He said he would think about it. I said, "Promise me you will." I kept a close watch on this inmate for a long time to see if he got depressed, but he was fine. In three days he told me that he had decided that since his wife and children were the only family he had in the world, he would forgive her, and try to make a go of it with her. The first thing that the staff told me in orientation was not to let any inmate get close to me, but as I look back on it, I will have to admit that this man got my sympathy, and my feelings for him were of a close nature. He had had polio as a child, which left him with a bad limp in his left leg, and he drug his left foot. Also, his left arm was bent at the elbow to a 90 degree angle, but he never complained when unloading a truck with 100 pounds. He never shirked his responsibility. He grabbed the bags just like everyone else, and grinned as he did his job. He never let staff or other inmates help him. When home after pulling the expiration of sentence, because he could not get a job for parole, (which was a requirement for parole release) I told him I wished him good luck, and wanted him not to return to this place. He assured me he would not be back.

Eighteen months later, one Saturday morning, someone knocked on my door. When I went to the door, it was this same inmate with his two children and his wife. I said "Ted, what is wrong?" He proceeded to tell me his family was hungry, and he had no money to feed them. My wife and I took them in and fed them. He was on his way from Texas to Tampa where he had a job waiting for him. He said the transmission in his old car went out in Mississippi, he took the radio out of the car, and swapped it to a junk yard dealer for a transmission, and replaced it himself. We never kept much cash money in the house. I asked him if $10 would get him enough gas to get to Tampa. He said it would, thanked me, and so far as I know, he is still well.

The other handicapped man was a completely different story. He was born with his right leg three inches shorter than the left one. It made him walk real bad wobbling from side to side. But I remember one day he came to the office walking as normal as everyone else. I asked him what had happened to him. He held up his right foot, and he had nailed three extra heels onto his State Brogans. I said, "Where did you get the extra heels?" He said, "I took them off of new shoes in the warehouse." I said, "Why didn't you get permission to go to the laundry, and get some old shoes to get the heels from?" He said, "I tried that and the laundry would not authorize it without a Doctor's prescription, and I said, to hell with that, I'll just steal some." I dropped the subject.

This is the same inmate that was accident-prone: smashed fingers, cut fingers, always getting hurt. It was the only time in my career that I intentionally falsified the grade sheet on a man to get rid of him. I was afraid he would get killed on my job. We had a grading system whereby each 3 months we graded the inmate on about 6 areas: work habits, attitude, learning ability, relationship with others, etc. We graded them from l to 5, No. 5 being outstanding, all the way down to number 1 being unsatisfactory. I graded this man #5 all the way so he could get paroled. I have never regretted it, neither have I ever admitted to it.

CHAPTER 4
TIME DRAGS ALONG

Some of the inmates had some crazy sentences, such as six months to life. I didn't understand the reasoning behind this kind of sentence, but as time went on, I could see the use of it. Each person with this sentence would see the parole officer each and every six months. It would work the parole officers to death seeing the men so often, and give them a lot of responsibility of not turning an inmate loose on society before he was ready. If he never got his mind right, he could spend his whole life in jail.

Sometimes, new laws like this would cause riots among the inmate population of an institution. One such riot unfurled right after work and evening meal. A gang of 125 inmates gathered up together in front of the dining hall and started to chant, "We are going to town." and they started toward the fence behind the powerhouse. The on-duty sergeant called the superintendent. He came on in because he just lived three houses outside the gate. The Lt. said, "I'm going to keep them off of the fence." As the gang went around the north side of the powerhouse, the Lt. went around the south side. They met on the east side. The Lt. had a loaded army 45 revolver in his hand. When they came face to face, the Lt. raised the gun, intending to fire over their heads.

He pulled the trigger, and the leader of the gang screamed and grabbed his head, and fell backwards into the crowd. The gang stopped in their tracks, turned and ran back up the hill behind the warehouse. They were one short, because their leader was shot dead, or so they thought. The Lt. who shot him, also thought he was dead. As a matter of fact, the bullet from the 45 had hit the inmate at the hairline, and just pealed back the hair and skin from the top of his head. The Lt. said, "I just scalped him." Lucky for all concerned, he was not hurt. The inmate was out of action, and wanted no more chanting and escaping. He was glad to be alive.

Meanwhile, the gang, going behind the warehouse, met a Sergeant who was carrying a 38 special. He was an old timer, and was not as compassionate as the Lt. He shot a little Mexican boy in the leg. The inmate grabbed his leg, and with blood running through his fingers, was told by another inmate, "My God, they're shooting real bullets." The gang turned and ran back around the chow hall, which was in the same building as the warehouse. They turned toward the east gate, and were running on the big double wide sidewalk, while still chanting "we're going to town." When they reached near the Quonset hut, they ran head on into the superintendent with a double barrel 12 gauge shotgun, loaded with "buckshot. Their new leader yelled, "it's only loaded with salt. It won't hurt you." The superintendent threw the shotgun up, and shot into the metal building, tearing a hole in the building the size of the softball. The rear of the gang kept shoving the front of the gang, yelling "Go, go go!" The superintendent lowered the barrel, and shot into the ground in front of the mob, not realizing that the walkway would bounce the flattened shot, and make it sail into the crowd. There was only 9 pellets in a 00 "buckshot shell. The concrete flattened the shot, and they sailed into 9 men, and mowed them down. Peace was restored immediately. There was a lot of crying, moaning, and groaning, but no more chanting "we are going to town". The A & B dorm, and C & D dorms faced each other right where the men were halted, and the superintendent yelled, "Unlock the doors to C & D dorms". Then, to the mob he yelled, "Get in the C & D dormitories right now!" I guess they believed now, that the superintendent and his men would kill them if they didn't do as they were told. It took most all the night to get the leaders sorted out, and put in confinement cells. Some of the correctional officers had been on duty for 14-16 hours. It was reported to me that the inmates in confinement would not settle down, and finally the superintendent threw tear gas to them. One of the officers said, "The cursing and foul language, and threats turned to crying and praying." One of the sergeants that had been on duty listening to all this crap said, "Now I'm getting my overtime pay, listening to these prayers and crying for mercy." The doctor that was paid to care for these inmates spent a good part of the night plucking and digging shot out of at least 12 inmates.

While we are on the subject of shooting, there is a happening I must tell you about. Inside the compound fence, there is a water tower and tank. It must be 300-400 feet tall. It's just inside the east gate, in front of the old control office. At one time, it got to be a popular pastime to climb up the ladder of the tank, and yell at all the inmates on the ground. Inmates did the climbing, and not the staff. One young lad decided to climb at the wrong time. Both the superintendent and the lieutenant were in a bad mood on this evening. The Lt. heard a lot of yelling and laughing, and went outside to investigate, and found an inmate all the way up on the catwalk yelling down to the crowd of inmates on the ground. The Lt. stepped back into the office and called the superintendent's house, and told him, "Sir, we have one on the water tank." He hung up the phone, went into the arsenal, got out a double barrel 12 gauge shotgun, and some #8 bird shot shells. By this time, the superintendent had arrived at the gate. The two of them walked out to the water tank, told the onlookers to go to the dormitories. Now here is where the facts get kind of cloudy, or foggy. The superintendent says he said, "I'm a good mind to shoot his ass off that tank." The Lt. said all I heard was, "Shoot his ass off the tank." Anyway, the Lt. threw up the shotgun, and aimed at the posterior of the inmate. He pulled the trigger.....BOOM!! Loud yell!!! Then, from the sky, the words were heard "Don't shoot anymore, I'm coming down." End of story. The reason you could say end of story back in those days was that the law of the superintendent, and the officer on duty was never questioned, or investigated by outsiders. But, to my knowledge, the popularity of climbing the water tank dwindled to zero immediately.

I remember when I went to work, there was a new captain who had just been hired. He was a green horn. He was educated in the college to the point of being honed to a keen edge. I knew the first time I saw him, he was a square peg in a round hole, or vice versa. Almost every correctional officer that we had was a local person, slightly red-necked, or at least pink. When you met one of these men, he would greet you with "hey" or "yep". This new captain would say, "Hello. How are you guys?" I think the thing that really got him was that one day we had an inmate to escape, which is a signal 6. They had every vehicle that had a radio in it, out patrolling all the roads for ten miles around ACI. One of the radios was causing static when it was on, so this green horn Capt. told all the vehicles to turn their radios off, and he would tell them one at a time to turn them back on. The one that comes on causing static, will be the problem. There was a big silence on the air. The assistant supt. came back from out of town, and when he got on the air with a 10-8, the control office told him of the signal 6. He joined in on the chase, but could not raise any of the vehicles by radio. He went looking for them and found one down the Gulf Power Road, and asked him if he had heard him calling on the radio. The officer said, "No." Assist. Supt. said, "Is your radio working?" The officer said, "Not right now, it's off." "Why?" asked the Supt. The officer said, "Because the Capt. told all of us to turn them off, and he would tell us when to turn them back on."

"I wonder how he is going to tell you that." The Supt. said. The chase officer said, "I've been wondering that myself. I thought maybe that was what you were doing out here, sir." Although, I have never heard of the Capt. since, I have heard the radio story mentioned several times at coffee break.

Prison guards in a youthful offender institution are called correctional officers, and not prison guards. I don't know why. I guess the title correctional officers has less brash to it. After all, we were supposed to correct these boys, not only guard them. There are good and bad officers. I know some I would not trust as far as I could throw them, but some I would trust with my life.

I can recall some funny things that happened concerning the crime investigations. I remember one day I was walking to the kitchen. The supervisor of kitchens told me he had a case before the investigation Lt. I asked what it was about. He said that he had an inmate who was prone to steal, and he was trying to break him of the habit. He had caught him stealing an apple from the cooler the day before, and had taken him to the Lt.'s office with the apple, and gave the Lt. the apple as evidence in the case. It was almost 4 pm. The morning Lt. put the apple in the desk drawer of the Lt.'s desk, and sent the inmate to the dorm, with instructions to report back to him in the AM for a trial. The kitchen man told me today, "I got my thief back with a phone call that the case had been nol-prossed, because of the loss of evidence." The second shift Lt. had eaten the evidence.

Tall tales and lies are abundant in the chain gang. I heard my share during my tenure at Apalachee Correctional Institution. I'm going to tell you some. I don't know whether they are true or not. You be the judge.

One night the person on duty at the powerhouse was so sleepy that he laid his head down on the desk and went to sleep. During his nap (which would cost him his job if caught) he heard a noise, opened his eyes, and saw a pair of shoes right in front of him. He said "Amen," and sat up straight.

Another time, we had a Lt. in security who looked just like Barney Fife on the Andy Griffith show. He was the funniest person on our staff. He told me one day back in the mid 70's, that on the weekday, he was on second shift. One morning he was cutting his grass. He had on old ragged clothes, and was cutting the grass close to the street. A lady in a fine car, evidently thought he was a yard boy who cut grass for a living, because she asked him, "What do you get for cutting yards?" His reply was, "This lady lets me sleep with her." Squealing tires could be heard for a block away. I don't know, like I said, how true this was, but I wouldn't put it past him. This was the same Lt. who ate the apple evidence.

This is true. When you get a bunch of men together, sparks will fly. Our purchasing agent was usually the one who took the brunt of the jokes. He was a man of means, but stingy. I have seen him smoke a pipe, and bang out the burnt ashes in an ashtray. He would pick out the unburned tobacco, and put them back into his pipe. I smoked the same kind of pipe at that time also: a semi-crook Kaywoody. The purchasing agent would ask me to fix his pipe, meaning he wanted me to clean it, and remount the bowl. So, I could get close to his pipe without suspicion. One day, the accountant came to me with a tiny bottle of red liquid, and told me it was a liquid to put on a child's thumb to keep them from sucking their thumb. He said, "Would you like to put some of this on the purchasing agent's pipe stem?" Well, it had been a pretty dull week so far, and I decided to liven it up a little. I went into the purchasing agent's office, sat down in a side chair, just as the purchasing agent went into the bathroom, leaving his pipe in the ashtray. I picked up his pipe, and rubbed some of the red liquid on his pipe. When he came out, I knew he would put that nasty old thing in his mouth, because he did not spend many minutes a day without it. Sure enough, when he got back, in his mouth it went. I looked through the window which was one whole wall, into the big office where all of us, except the purchasing agent worked. I saw the accountant looking at us. The purchasing agent took the pipe out and looked at it. Of course, he didn't see anything wrong. He licked his lips, frowned, and said, "I'm going to have to change tobacco. That Granger is getting to taste terrible." He went back into the toilet to wash his mouth and hands off, leaving his pipe in the ashtray again. I just reached up and got his pipe again, and gave it another dose of red liquid. I saw the accountant laughing like crazy. I motioned for him to cool it. When the purchasing agent came back in, he took his pipe, and banged it against the top of a trash can, turned to me and said, "You got any fresh Granger?" "Sure" I said, handing him my fresh pack of tobacco.

He filled his pipe, and lit it. He got the same effect, only worse. He said, "Yours is worse than mine." I replied, "I wondered if it was me that was crazy." He took his pipe into the bathroom, and washed it off saying, "It may be this old pipe. I have had it for years." When he came out, and put the pipe into the ashtray again, he went back into the bathroom again to wash his hands. I doused his pipe again. The staff in the office, by now, had all quit work, and were standing around watching us. The purchasing agent would not touch the pipe any more, so I went back to my desk, and after a while, I gave the little bottle of red stuff back to the accountant. He just dropped the bottle into his shirt pocket. When I saw him do that, I said, "Oh boy, oh boy!" A light bulb came on in my mind. I waited until lunch time. One of the clerk officers always went with our inmates to check them in. As soon as the inmates were gone, I went into the purchasing agent's office, and said, "Old friend, I think I have found your problem with your pipe. Just go out there, and stand by the accountant. Put your hand on his shoulder, lean over and look down into his shirt pocket."

Let me give you a description of these two characters: the accountant was 6'2" tall, weighing 250 pounds. The purchasing agent was 58 years old, compared to the acct.'s age of 25. The purchasing agent weighed 160 pounds, and stood 5'9" tall. When the purchasing agent looked in the accountant's pocket, (Wow, if I had known what would have happened, I never would have done what I did) the purchasing agent doubled up his fist, and struck the giant of a man in the side of his face with all his might. The accountant was still sitting down when the blow struck him. He was sitting in a typist's chair with no arms. As the old saying goes, there was only two blows struck, the purchasing agent first struck the side of the accountant's head, and the accountant's butt struck the floor. The acct. said, "Man, have you lost your mind?" The purchasing agent said, "Pay back!"

Later on that week, the accountant told the purchasing agent, "Gilley was the one who put that hot stuff on your pipe." The purchasing agent replied, "Gilley is my friend, and would not do anything like that. If you say anything like that again, I'll bop you again." I was hearing all of this, and when the purchasing agent looked my way, I just winked. Now, I can tell this story, because both the purchasing agent, and the accountant, who were both named Charlie, were dear friends, and have passed away. My life is now missing a big chunk of good fellowship.

The purchasing agent was a good friend, and trusted me all the way. I have never seen a person like him that felt that I could do anything like him. I remember one day I was inventorying the warehouse and he came back where I was counting inmate shoes. He sat down on a soap drum and said, "I have a party to attend tonight. A real classy political party, and I look so shaggy. Can you cut my hair for me?" I put down my kardex file and said, "Why, sure I will be glad to cut your hair." We had some barber scissors, comb and drip cloth. I thought, boy, I am going to scalp him, but when I looked him in the face, I couldn't do it. I had never cut anyone's hair before in my life, but I had seen it done. I acted like a barber and said, "Do you want a full cut, or just a trim?"

"Just a trim", he answered. Forty five minutes later, I took an inmate's razor out of stock and trimmed his neck. He was my buddy forever more. He never knew that his hair was the first I ever cut, and the last too, in fact.

I don't mean to rave on about the purchasing agent, but he is the best character I know to write about. He was as vain a man as I ever saw. He had a bookcase with glass sliding doors in his office. He would sit in his executive chair, rare back, with his legs crossed, and stare at his own reflection for hours at a time. He was not nearly as handsome as I, but I would not dare to inform him of this fact!

The purchasing agent kept his thinning gray hair slicked back, and he would not permit anyone to touch his hair. There was a young clerk that I think was some kin to the purchasing agent. One afternoon, the young clerk came over to my desk, pulled a chair up real close so no inmates could hear and said, "When the inmates leave out today, the purchasing agent always goes out into the closet to throw all the breakers, turning out the lights. When he does, the accountant and I will grab him, and hold him. You come in and rub the purchasing agent's head, and really mess up his hair." I thought to myself, I wasn't born yesterday, and didn't fall off of a cabbage truck when I came to town. But, I said "O.K." not actually believing that those two would be that foolish. Just as soon as the inmates were out of sight, the purchasing agent went into the closet to pull the lights. The two of them went in behind him. When the big accountant bear-hugged him, he could not get away, but the little clerk was in front of him. The purchasing agent was kicking him, and he looked like a blanket flapping in the breeze. All the time he was yelling, "Come on Gilley! Rub his head!" The little clerk kept yelling this at me while I was yelling, "Hold him men, hold him men!" I was all the way across the office out in the hall, laughing and yelling "Hold him!" When they finally turned the purchasing agent loose, the clerk said, "Cliff, why didn't you rub his head?" I only replied, "My mother did not raise a fool."

When I began my work with finance and supply (that is what our department was called), the business manager's office was in our office, but before long he moved his office down to the little temporary white wooden building just inside the east gate which was also the control office. I never did understand why he moved, or why the superintendent moved him. All of his employees and inmates were half-way across the 15 acre compound, but the purchasing agent inherited the job as office manager which made the next incident possible. The inmate canteen was also down close to the east gate. The Eli Witt Company out of Quincy, Florida was one of the big suppliers of tobacco and candy products for the canteen. The old man that delivered the candy and tobacco would drive up the hill, come into the business office and on into the purchasing agent's office which used to be the business manager's office. I never knew why he came all the way up there, unless it was to brown nose the purchasing agent. Anyway, on this particular day, I saw him come in and walk right in front of my desk, and I noticed he had a 12-pack of Reese's Peanut Butter cups in his hand. He went on into the purchasing agent's office, and stayed about 15 minutes. When he came out he said, "Share the candy with your help out here." I thought that was a nice gesture, especially since we processed the invoices for his company, and ordered the products for the canteen. We even wrote the checks for it, mailing them to his firm.

Two whole walls of the purchasing agent's office were glass starting at 30 inches from the floor and going to the ceiling. There was strictly no privacy in the office. On this day, as soon as the Eli Witt man left, I watched the purchasing agent. He got up from the desk with the box of candy in his hand, and went into the closet where the safe was. Just a minute or two later, I heard the safe door slam. I thought to myself, that stingy old codger is going to keep all of that candy for himself. I began to consider all of my options. No one except the purchasing agent, and the business manager knew the combination to the safe. Wait a minute, the purchasing agent had told me he had to be off the next day. Wheels began to turn in my crafty old head. That afternoon, on the way out to the gate, the purchasing agent kept talking about his grandson, and how happy he was when the purchasing agent brought him some candy. I thought, you are not going to take our candy home to that grandson.

The next day I called the business manager and told him I had some vending machine money I needed to put in the safe, and would he come open the safe for me. No hesitation, he just came up and opened the safe. He came by my desk and said, "The safe is open, Mr. Gilley." I went to the safe, took out the box of Reese's cups, took out 11 cups, and left one. On the inside bottom of the box I wrote, "The Phantom has struck". I took the 11 Reese's cups out into the big office, and passed out the candy with a word of warning, "You ain't ever had no Reese's cup." Every person including the inmates knew what the story was. You can't keep a secret from convicts. When the purchasing agent came back to work, he missed the candy, and as I supposed, he came straight to me. He said, "Someone broke into the safe, and stole my candy." I said to him, "Are you sure it was yours that he stole? Only one of the Reese's cup was yours, according to the Eli Witt man. He left it for you to give to your help, isn't that right?" "Yes," he said, "but now, I can't give it out." "Don't worry about it, these helpers of yours don't mind." The purchasing agent said, "I want to know who it was that got into the safe." I said, "Look around you. Just how many people in here know the combination to the safe?" He said, "None of them." I said, "Who has the combination?" He said, "Only me and the boss." I said, "A wee ha! That tells you who the phantom is." He gave no reply, just deep thought, and then he said, "I don't believe it."

This you may not believe, but it is gospel. The same man from Eli Witt came in with a handful of double wide book matches, laid them on the purchasing agent's desk. The purchasing agent picked them up, and put them in the top right-hand drawer of the desk. I waited until the purchasing agent went out of his office. I went in and got all the book matches, and left a note, "The Phantom strikes again." The funny part of this is, that the State of Florida furnished all the book matches you could use for free. In fact, when I took the double wide matches, there was half a book of matches in the same drawer. The purchasing agent just could not resist something that was free.

CHAPTER 5
FROM COST TO EQUIPMENT

I was given a 10% raise and given the job of equipment manager. That was a newly-created job until this day in reference. I had to go back into all the records, pull out all capital outlay expenditures, and make equipment cards for everything that had a value of at least $25, and a life expectancy of one year. Boy, what a job: all telephones, fire extinguishers, drills, and saws. There were about 3,000 pieces of equipment by the time I got caught up. When I began to get caught up on entering the equipment record, I began to get curious as to how we got by the auditing department. When I looked up the auditing report for the previous years, I found three big words "NO RECORDS KEPT". I think these audit reports had a great deal of influence on establishing my new job. When I read the manual on capital outlay, I learned that I had to inventory each piece of equipment once a year, I had to verify each time I found the equipment, and make a notation on the card of the date and location found. My first inventory was quite interesting. The department heads had been coasting for so long, they didn't know, nor did they care where their equipment was. I finally got tired of being brushed off, and ignored, when I told a department head he was missing a piece of equipment. So, I went over the purchasing agent, and business manager's heads all the way to the superintendent. I was told by some of the department heads that the superintendent reminded them of the director of education that was fired because he could not find a typewriter. From that day onward, I got plenty of respect. I worked the equipment manager's job until I had been working 13 years. After I had been on the job for 10 years, I had three sets of equipment cards. One by department, one by numerical ACI order, and one by location.

In the year 1970, my business manager called me into his office to discuss a procedure change. Tallahassee central office said if we would send a copy of all our equipment cards to them, they would put them on computer printout, and we could destroy all the rest of our cards. When we wanted a printout, all we had to do was call them. We would receive it in the mail the next day. I said, "Bull! I will not destroy any of my records for the past five years. I have received outstanding audit reports. I will let them keep records for us, but I'm going to maintain my records as in the past." Well, I sent them a copy of all our equipment and capital outlay, and fixed asset cards.

When audit time and closing annual reports were due, I called them for a printout, but I started one inmate on typing an inventory list for the auditor. It took the inmate three days to type the list. Meanwhile, I was working on balancing my recapitulation sheet.

Every penny of capital and fixed assets spent appeared on the recapitulation sheet, and it balanced with the accountant's records of funds spent. That recapitulation sheet was something I came up with on my own to be sure I didn't overlook any expenditure for new equipment.

Well, the auditor came and wanted to see the computer printout from Tallahassee. I told him I had requested one a month earlier, but had no response from them. The reply I got from the auditor was, "What do you expect?" Then he said, "I hope you didn't destroy your records as instructed." I said, "No, and that ain't the half of it. I ain't going to."

There was one thing that happened that was worth telling. On July 1st,1959, the Florida State Hospital had a farm just west of the ACI compound run by the Hospital, using black prisoners. The legislature decided to have the farm turned over to ACI since prisoners were already there. Transfer of records, equipment and buildings would be transferred at no cost. It fell my lot to make the transfer. I met with the Florida State Hospital equipment manager, and we made the transfer. When the auditors checked the records, and transfer, they gave us each an "atta-boy". Things rocked along for six months, and we had to replace a motor in the powerhouse boiler room. I got the invoice voucher, and prepared a plant ledger posting to enter the cost of the motor to the building. and survey the new motor at estimated worth. Well, when I reached over to pull out the building card, there was not one. I went back, pulled the transfer of capital outlay, and found to my chagrin, there was no transfer of the boiler room. I remember now that the cost was $54,000. "Well," I said, "There goes my only atta-boy. What now?" I just went back, and added the building, not changing the total, just added the boiler room onto the next year with a plant ledger, as if it was a new purchase. I crossed my fingers, and hoped for a near-sighted audit next time. The next year, when the auditor checked the records, he never noticed a thing. One more "atta-boy"!

Three weeks ago now, we were at the grave site burying the business manager that I have been talking about when a familiar-looking man came up to me and said, "Do you remember me, Mr. Gilley?" I looked and said, "Yes, of course. Auditing department of Marianna, Florida." I hadn't seen him for 10 years. It brought back good memories.

The auditors played an important role in state government. I never minded them checking my work. That is what they are paid to do. I always tried to do my job the best I could. All the auditors I ever met liked to find everything in order. I even had one to tell me one time that he was auditing the port authority of Jacksonville, and they were missing a huge freighter. He said he leaned back in his chair with hands clasped behind his head, and said, "A hundred years from now, who will know."

One day one of the auditors that was auditing capital outlay expenditures, couldn't get the amount of departments and grand total to balance. He asked me about it. I said, "Just a minute." I reached down to the bottom right hand drawer, and pulled out a 40 line, 25-space across legal pad, and unfolded it across my desk. He said, "Good Lord, what's that?" I replied, "recapitulation sheet." He said, "I never saw one of those." I said, "Oh, it's not legal, or mandatory. I just concocted it up myself for my own benefit. Now, give me a voucher number." "I don't have one" he said I said, "How about a plant ledger number?" "Don't have one", he said. "How about vendor name?" I asked. "Don't have one", he said. I said, "Oh #$%^ what do you have?" He said, "Two figures that don't match." I said, "Give me the total difference of the two." He said, "$256." I ran my finger down the sheet of expenditures, and said, "Overhead projector, education department, new purchased voucher #132." "Man, I've been looking for that for three hours. Why didn't you give me that when I started capital outlay?" "You didn't ask", I said. "I don't have to do this you know. But, when I get this grand total to match that figure you've got right there," (pointing to grand total expenditures he got from accountant's record), "Then I know I've got it right!" I said. We had the same auditor every year, and this auditor would say to me, "Mr. Gilley, let me see your recapitulation of capital and fixed outlay." I saw him one day just copying off of my recap. sheet. Jokingly I said, "Are you just copying my audit report?" "Of course not!" he said, grinning.

While I was equipment manager, I had a model 99 calculator. It was electric/manual. No modules, no electrodes, you just push a key, and all hell broke loose inside that housing. But, that thing taught me how: to be patient, and keep my temper, forget four-letter words, how not to yell or scream, be oblivious to loud calculators, and how to work with diligence. I grew to love that old monster. When it was in adjustment, it would print out some of the prettiest tapes you ever saw. Now, for years on end, Osment

Business Machines had the contract for the repairs on the old 99. The repairman was something to watch. When he took the cover off my machine, the whole office would stop and come over to watch. I would tell him to make a loud division on the machine. He would divide 100 by 33. That thing would wiggle, hop and dance all over the desk for five minutes. The business manager was ashamed of the 99, and offered to get me an electronic one, but I didn't want one of those. People who had electronic ones had their calculators confiscated when they were away from their desks. No one ever confiscated mine. It was too heavy. It weighed about 40 pounds. A week ago, I was searching through a junk drawer. Don't everyone have a junk drawer? If you don't have one, please get one! It is a real experience to rumble in it when you get bored. My junk drawer is 42 years old last May 5th. The reason I remember is because we moved into this house on our fifth wedding anniversary. Boy, can I chase rabbits!! Well, anyway, while digging in the junk drawer, I saw this little wrench. It is open-ended about two inches long, 5/32" and 5/16" on the other end. It is the cutest little wrench I ever saw. When I picked it up, memories flooded my mind, back to the old 99 model Remington calculator. The wrench was left laying on my desk the last time that man worked on my calculator. I said I would save it for him until he came back. Two weeks later, Mr. Osment told me my repairman had suddenly died with a heart attack. He was only 48 years old, so I kept the wrench. It's laying here just a few inches from my paper. That has been 35 years ago, and the wrench has never been used in all that time.

While I was equipment manager, I acquired the reputation of being able to fix anything, and I could fix a lot of things. I remember the purchasing agent said to me, "I have a 12 gauge automatic shotgun I want you to check because it jams every time I shoot it. I want you to look at it and tell me what to do about it." He brought it to his office. At that time, we had moved into the new administration building. November '68 was moving date. Well, he called me into his office, gave me the gun and three live shells. I should have known better, but I put one of the shells in the gun, and got the gun by the barrel, and pressed down the way a barrel does when it fires. Well, it fired off in the purchasing agent's office. I made sure no one was in the way. I shot a hole in the Celotex over the purchasing agent's head. The shot hit the concrete deck in the roof, and the shot rained down on the accountant next door. I had not noticed him, but the officer in the control room who thought he was a gun mechanic, came in, walked up behind me, and was looking over my shoulder when the gun went off. I turned and saw him going out the door without being told to get out of the way. The people across the hall and people in our own offices didn't even hear the shot. I threw my coat over the shotgun and took it to my car, and locked it up in the trunk. In case you are interested in what happened about the gun jamming, well, it had me buffaloed. I was lucky the next day while I was in a local hardware store, I heard a man talking who was a Remington Arms salesman. I introduced myself, and asked how long he would be there. He said, "one hour." I told him I had a gun and wanted him to look at it. I rushed home and got the gun. When he saw it, he said, "Where did you get this gun?" I said, "It isn't mine, and I don't know where it came from." He said, "The gun is perfect, the only thing is, you have to shoot 2-1/2" shells in it. I only know of one store that has any 2-1/2" shells, and he has only 1/2 a case. All the guns you are familiar with use 2 3/4" shells don't they?" I said "Yes." He said, "You have you a real collector's item there. I've only seen one other like that." I carried it back to the purchasing agent and told him to collect this gun, or find him a collector and sell it to him. He didn't know whether to be happy or mad. I don't know what he ever did with the gun.

Shortly after we moved into our new office space, I was called into the purchasing agent's office and advised that the afternoon would be spent doing a shake-down. I said, "O.K. fine. I'll be ready." We had not really had a good shakedown since we had moved. I figured it was a general shakedown looking for any kind of contraband. But, when we got back from lunch, we were told the purchasing agent's inmate secretary had bee accused of selling dope to the other inmates. They thought that it was hidden in the office. We spent about three hours looking in ceiling light sockets, in desk drawers, file cabinets, and other drawers with no luck. Finally one other officer said, "Wait a minute." He pulled the center drawer all the way out, and held it up high to look under the bottom of the drawer. He said, "Bingo!" There taped to the bottom of the drawer was a little cellophane package with two capsules. Every drawer in his desk had dope taped to the back and bottom of them. When we got all the stuff gathered up, we called him in. He said it was not dope. It was only glycerin. You could buy it in the grocery store. For 50 tablets it would only cost $3.50. He was selling these for $.50 for a package of two or in exchange for a pack of cigarettes. We turned him over to the security department for handling. Needless to say, we never saw him again. They decided he could best pull his time at Raiford State Prison. He did admit that his mother brought the pills to him on visiting day. He said women take the glycerin to harden their nails, and some of the dumber inmates would take them and get high as a kite, thinking they were taking uppers.

CHAPTER 6
BANKING AND FINANCE

It is a different world inside those fences. It is hard to believe when you see all 450 of these young men, and not a single one has a penny in his pocket. Money was contraband at ACI. Any caught with cash money, the money was taken and deposited in the inmates' canteen fund or the revolving fund. The way the system worked, was that each inmate had a bank account, and money received by the institution for the inmates' use was put into his checking account. The inmate canteen started with two cases of cokes and grew from that to a multi-thousand dollar business a week. The canteen purchased food, drinks, and various approved items, and sold them to inmates at approximately 20% markup. The profit at that time when I started my career was put into the inmate welfare fund. It was welfare, such as musical instruments, ball gloves, bats, and things to entertain inmates during their off -duty time.

Now, this is where the catch comes in. How does the inmate purchase the items out of the canteen: if they had money in their account in the bank, the education department printed checks for them just like in the outside world. It is the inmate's responsibility to keep up with the amount he has in his account.

The canteen is open right after work at 5:00 p.m. until all who want to spend have had at least one chance. There is a limit of $5.00 per week for each inmate. Things went pretty well for a while with the honor system. I knew it couldn't last. Before long, we were getting 4-6 bogus checks a day. Someone smarter than I suggested that we require each inmate to write his check at the time of purchase at the canteen in front of the officer in charge of the canteen, and put his thumbprint of his right hand with black ink on his check. That worked for a while, no bogus checks. Then one day, the canteen accountant said, "We got a forgery." The purchasing agent said, "Do you have a print?" "Oh yeah." was the reply. "Let's send it to Tallahassee and get it identified." We did, and received a call from the laboratory in Tallahassee with a question, "What are you guys trying to pull over there? This is not a thumbprint. It is a toe print of a big toe on a left foot. The only way I could identify it would be for you to send me the print of every man's left big toe." Well, the superintendent had gotten in on it by now, and he said, "Do it. I want that man." Well, we started eliminating all the men that could not have been at the canteen the night before. Some were on duty, some sick, some not eligible. We wound up with about 150 men we needed to print. We got started on them, bringing them in one at a time to the purchasing agent's office, and making them pull off their left shoe and sock, putting their big toe print on half a sheet of typing paper with their name. We had only gotten about 25 done when an inmate came in and was told to take off his left shoe and sock. He said, "No, that won't be necessary. I did it. I never knew you guys would be so chincey over a mere $5.00." I said, "The amount was not that important, but you have committed a felony because our inmate bank is certified." It sounded good, but I really didn't know whether we were certified or not. I said, "Tell me how you got your shoe and sock off and put your foot up on the counter without the officer seeing you?" He said, "I knew the prices of everything, so I chose the items to total $5.00. I wrote a check for $5.00 on the second check in my checkbook leaving the top one blank, took a magic marker and put ink on my big toe, and placed a print on the second check. When I ordered all I was going to get, it amounted to $5.00, and the officer told me to make a check for $5.00. I put a thumbprint on the first check, picked up my checkbook and tore out the second check so slick that the officer didn't notice that I gave him a toe-printed check."

They carried the inmate to court, and he pled guilty. The judge in Marianna gave him three additional years for forgery and passing a bad check. Anyway, he was no longer a first offender, and was transferred back to Raiford State Prison.

I learned early that inmates have different beliefs than we officers do. One day I walked back through the warehouse. I always wore shoes with rubber soles so I could walk quietly. As I rounded the corner, I saw movement on top of a bunch of cases of Corn Flakes. I eased on around and looked up and there was an inmate with an individual box of Corn Flakes open, stuffing them in his mouth. I called him by name and told him to get down and bring the evidence with him. I took him into the purchasing agent's office and told him I wanted to borrow his desk and office for a crime investigation. I told the purchasing agent he could stay and be a witness. I left the inmate standing. I turned the big executive's chair around and looked up at him. I said in the most judicial voice I could muster, "Do you know what you have done?" He said, "Yeah." "Don't you mean, yes sir?" I barked at him. "Yes sir, that is what I meant to say, but you scared the hell out of me with that tough voice." "O.K." I said, "Let's start over. Do you know you are stealing?" "Oh no" he replied, "How do you figure?" I roared. "These are my Corn Flakes." he said. He said, "In the breakfast line in the morning, they were going to give me this box of Corn Flakes, so I decided to eat mine today." "How about that man in the kitchen last week that they shot down for stealing a quart of peanut butter? Was that stealing?" He replied by saying, "Oh yes, sir." I asked, "How do you figure?" "Well, I just took what was mine. He took a whole lot of the other inmates' stuff. He never could eat all that peanut butter." he said. The purchasing agent was sitting over there in a side chair. When I looked over there he had his head turned away from the inmate with one eyebrow raised up and one eye closed, trying to keep from at least snickering, and with an expression saying, "What now judge?" I started to throw something at him, and would have if we had been alone. I turned to the inmate and said, "Don't steal anymore! Now, get out of here!" I had always prided myself that I could discipline my inmates without sending them to confinement or the work squad. The only man I sent to discipline action by a write up was a minor incident, but I was angry and didn't want to do something that I would regret later or be disciplined myself for. What happened was, I had managed to beg the authorities out of a new typist's chair. Most of our furniture was war surplus. I got a new chair which was comfortable as well as pretty. When I got it I told everybody out loud, "While I'm out inventorying, or for any reason, they could use my new chair, but when I came in, whoever had their butt in my chair should move it and put it back where it belonged." Well, one day, I came in and a little blonde kid with a bad attitude toward the staff and other inmates, was in my chair. But the way he acted, you couldn't really write him up for it. When I called his name, he was across the office sitting in my chair, and when I called his name, he glared at me, stood up, and knocked my chair all the way across the office, even past my desk. I thought O.K. boy, you are mine now. We had a no smoking rule for our inmates during working hours. I knew this man had been going to the library to checkout a book every day. I suspected he was going down there to smoke. They allowed smoking in the library. That afternoon when he got his permit signed by his supervisor to go to the library, I gave him a few minutes, and followed him. When I walked in the library, there he was smoking. I just stopped and glared at him. Then I gave him a smirk, and a grin of revenge and walked back to my office. I wrote him up on a discipline report recommending that he be reassigned to poultry or brick plant which were hard work jobs. I never saw him again.

In orientation, when I first came to work and someone was talking about ""new cocked"," I asked what that meant? I was told that it meant tricked. I foolishly replied, "There ain't an inmate that ever was born that could 'new cock' me." The people that heard me say that said nothing, they just grinned. I hadn't been at work more than a month and I was in the warehouse when the freight truck left a package. I opened it and saw that it was ether.

We kept this locked up in the safe, and when a diesel engine wouldn't crank, you gave the carburetor a shot of that stuff and it would start every time. Well, I locked all ten cans up in the safe." About a month later, the business manager was out walking among clothing bins, and saw a little opening between two pair of pants. He ran his hand into the hole and came out with a can of that ether. He came and gave it to me. I said, "Someone has found out the combination to the safe because I had locked all of the tin cans up in the safe." The can had not been opened, so I put it back in the safe and forgot the incident, but I didn't forget that I must have been ""new cocked"". Three months later, one of the better inmates came to me and said, "Mr. Gilley, I want to tell you about that can of ether. You remember when you received it, and turned to go. An inmate came up to you on the opposite side from the box of cans sitting by your foot and asked you to sign a store's requisition that a maintenance man was waiting on?" I said, "Yes." He said, "(an inmate's name) who passed by you and bent down and picked a can up, and stuck it into his shirt and kept right on walking." I asked, "Why didn't you tell me then when he did it?" He said, "Mr. Gilley, I have to live with these guys. If it had been life threatening to you, I would have told you. He thought that stuff was good for sniffing, but no one would buy the stuff, and they know not to sniff it, so they just hid it." So much for never being ""new cocked"."

Around the middle of 1960, one day, we got a signal 6 (escapee) from the soap factory. That was a little shack of a building between the maintenance shop and the powerhouse. The alarm was sounded at 5:15 pm. One man short at count time. A search was made at the soap factory with no luck. The bloodhounds were called out and circled the exterior fence twice. No luck there either. A full chase was initiated covering a 10-mile radius from the institution which lasted for three days. No one had seen a single suspicious person. The soap factory manager came to the Lieutenant's office on the third day and reported that an inmate had told him the signal 6 was in a hole in the ground under the floor of the soap factory. The manager asked the security to go search it out after count check. They did, and sure enough, there the escapee was.

He had raised up a piece of plywood from the floor, and dug a hole while the manager was out. He was taking the dirt out behind the powerhouse and scattering it on the ground so it wouldn't look suspicious. He had a helper during the three day ordeal to bring him food from the kitchen. There was a bathroom at the shack, so he could have lasted a week or more. At night, he would come out and sleep in the soap factory on a pile of rags. They could not charge him with escape, for he had not even left his place of work. I know they charged him with attempted escape, and knowing our Superintendent, he found some other charges to put on him besides that.

It didn't take me long to learn that there were two factors at ACI, the inmates and the enemy (the staff). Anything that the inmate can do to make life miserable for the enemy, the inmate is honor bound to see that it is done.

I heard two inmates talking one day. One said to the other inmate, "If you don't cool it, a free man will shoot you out of the saddle, and you will bust the gator wide open." I said to the inmate standing next to me, "What did he say?" The answer went like this, "He told that other man that if he didn't start acting right, an officer would write him up on a discipline report, and he would go straight to confinement." I said, "He didn't say that." Then I thought about it and said, "Yeah, I guess he did." The interpreter said, "Mr. Gilley, that is chain gang talk!" From that time on, I started learning "chain gang talk". In five years, I could hear it, and talk it also. But, I seldom ever had a need to talk it.

After working for the chain gang, I got so I could see some humor in almost any situation. For instance, one day I was working my kardex on the checkout counter right in front of the big roll up door, when some movement in the street behind the warehouse got my attention. When I looked up, there was an inmate passing by with a new 2X4 about 10 feet long over his shoulder, just poking along going west toward poultry. I learned later that he walked right through the west gate, being seen by more than one security guard. They, like I, thought he was going to poultry to do some carpentry work. When he got to poultry, he just kept poking along. The people at poultry thought he was going to the west unit to do some work with his 2X4. What else would he be doing with his 2X4? When he got to the west unit, which sat off the road far enough, that they couldn't see him, he kept right on poking toward the city of Sneads. As soon as he hit the highway 90, he threw away his escape aid, Mr. 2x4, and went on down the highway. When I heard what had happened, I didn't tell anyone I had been "new cocked". Two weeks later, the inmate was picked up in Pensacola, Florida.

During the time that ACI was on the honor system, (they called it minimum security) we spent hundreds of hours on manhunts. The surrounding communities were aware of our policy of awarding any person who was responsible for the apprehension of an escapee, a $25 reward. People were glad to assist in keeping criminals off the streets as well as getting a free check. One day a farmer from up in Georgia, which is just a couple of miles away, drove up to the control office in a pickup truck with a cattle body on his truck, and six inmates inside of it. He went up to the checkout window and asked, "You got some inmates out?" "Yes," the officer replied. "How many?" the farmer asked. "Seven," replied the officer. "Well" the farmer replied, "I've got six of them. Where do you want them? I'll take my $150 now please." The officer said, "Just line them up out there in the street and come on inside. We'll have to have your name and address so we will know where to send your check. The farmer turned around, took out his keys, and unlocked the gate to the cattle truck. He told the inmates to get out of his truck. An officer asked him how he kept the inmates from climbing out of the sides of the truck. The farmer said, "I drove 70 miles per hour all the way here. They were afraid to climb up ten feet off the ground, so I just didn't stop until I got here with them"

I heard an inmate say one time, "I don't mind those bloodhounds, and German police catch dogs. I could throw them off the trail with black pepper. It's those darn farmers with the double barrel shotguns that I dread. They are blood-thirsty and greedy for that reward money."

The public people were a great help in keeping those boys rounded up. I remember one day we received a call from the city police in Chattahoochee advising they had captured an inmate on the Booster Club Road. Some local citizen had seen an inmate in a blue shirt and blue pants climb out from under a semi-truck where he had been riding on the axle. When captured and questioned, he had crawled onto the axle of a Swift and Co. truck delivering meat to the kitchen at ACI. He had his name tag shirt on, and the police called our control office and asked if a man by this name was one of our inmates. The roster checked that he was on duty cleaning cans out back of the kitchen. When told this, the police said, "No more, he ain't. He is in jail at Chattahoochee in our way. Come get him." This was an easy chase. Some are not so easy.

I came to work one morning to hear this story the first thing. Just after dark the night before, the phone rang in the control room. It was the police department in Tallahassee, Florida, and they asked if we had a John Doe (a fictitious name). The officer checked his roster and told the caller, we did not have a man by that name. Tallahassee thanked our officer and hung up. In a few minutes the same officer called back. He said, "John Doe says he was in the west unit." The control officer relayed the call to the Lieutenant on duty at the west unit. When asked if he had a John Doe, the Lieutenant said, "Yes, we have him." The Tallahassee officer said, "No, you don't have him. I picked him up on breaking and entering just an hour ago." The officer said, "You are mistaken. We have him here. He is in confinement, and my Sergeant just checked confinement and he is asleep in his bed. Thanks," he said, and hung up. A few minutes later, the same policeman from Tallahassee called and asked to speak to the west unit Lieutenant. This time he told our Lt. "Go yourself. Get in the cell and pull the cover back.'" Three minutes later, the Lt. came back and said, "I'm on your side now. You do have my John Doe, and I have a pillow and towel with a pair of shoes. What are you going to do with him?" TPD said, "If you will come get him, you can have him. I feel sure you will give him justice. I know you want to know how he got out of the bars on the window in confinement. You ready for this? He used the handle of his spoon with toothpaste rubbed on the spoon, and rubbed the spoon handle on the bottom of the bar. The toothpaste has enough abrasive factor, that after 28 days of rubbing the bar, he cut all the way through it, pulled the bar, and bent it at the top until he could slip through. He walked over to the west side of the fence, climbed over the fence, and walked to highway 90, caught a ride with a person traveling from California to Jacksonville. He got off at Tallahassee and broke into a home with a silent burglar alarm, and within three hours he was back in jail. And, by the way, he wore out three spoon handles, and five tubes of toothpaste in 28 days. A huge price to pay for three hours of freedom.

Sometime around 1971, we had an inmate to run from the brick plant in Chattahoochee. They thought that he went down the river bank toward Blountstown. When this happens, the authority at ACI will send out an officer with the bloodhounds to track them down. On this day, the officer in charge of the bloodhounds was off duty. They got a buddy of mine who was an assistant coach at the institution along with two inmates. They sent them down to Flat Creek at Aspalaga Landing to look for tracks and search for clues. The two hounds acted very excited, and the officer found some footprints, or so he said, and they led right into the swamp. The five of them (including dogs) struck out right into the worst swamp in the county. After several hours of searching, they lost the trail. The man could have crossed the river anywhere, and they were miles from the point where they entered the swamp. But the officer came to a familiar spot in the swamp because he was a member in the River Junction Hunting Club, and this spot (inside the club) was known as Roger's hitching ground. There was a logging road that ran to the spot. Many years ago, a family named Rogers used to drive a buggy or wagon down to this point from their home in Mt. Pleasant, Florida, hitch up their team of mules or horses, and walk to the river to fish. Thus, it got it's name. This day I was working at my desk and my phone rang, and it was the control room. The Sergeant there told me that the assistant coach had called him and told him to call Gilley. He knows where Roger's hitching ground is, and tell him to come get me. The control officer told me to go out front, and a correctional officer would be there in a pickup truck ready to take me wherever I wanted to go. We headed out, and met the coach, two inmates, and two bloodhounds 1/4 mile from the hitching ground. The coach got in the cab with me and the driver. The inmates and dogs got in the back of the pickup truck. As soon as he got in, he asked me, "Where is the water jug?" I said, "I didn't bring any water." "Man," he said, "I'm starving for water." I said, "Why didn't you get you a drink at the hitching ground out of the creek?" He said, "I ain't drinking out of no creek." I said, "You ain't drinking out of no pickup truck today either." He said, "Man, I ain't never going to call for you to come get me again." I said, "Aw, hush, You are breaking my heart!"

Another tale, but true, I came home to my wife and told her we had an escaped inmate loose from the brick plant, which is on the same side of the river that we lived. The institution was across the big Apalachicola River, and very seldom did one escape from the institution and cross the river over to our county. But, when they escape from the brick plant, or River Junction Correctional Institution at the Florida State Hospital, that was a different story.

That night, the ladies in the WMU of the Calvary Baptist Church, which my wife and I attended, were meeting and the preacher was not living in the pastorium which was on the same plot with the church.

The ladies, a total of 9, were told that an inmate was loose, and to be careful. They locked the doors, proceeded with their program, and one lady was responsible for the refreshments. They had coffee and cookies. They were finished and were all standing around with a cup of coffee, and the lady that was the refreshment hostess, went back into the kitchen for something, and opened the door to the bottom row of cabinets. There inside the cabinet, she saw a man's feet. She slammed the cabinet doors shut, went into the main room where the women were standing with their coffee. She told them, "There is a man in the kitchen cabinets." Just like fireworks going off, all nine of the women went out the

55

door at the same time. My wife's car was closest to the door. My wife was the smallest in the crowd, and the slowest, all 8 of the other women had crowded into our car, and no room was left for her to drive. Finally, the women that had driven their own cars, were encouraged to get into their cars to leave. When my wife was finally able to get her car going, she thought of a highway patrol officer that lived down the road a short way. She stopped at his house, and told him what had happened. He jumped in his patrol car, and drove to the church. Of course, the man had heard the excitement, and had left by then. The patrol officer notified the dispatcher of the sighting, and they contacted ACI. Just on a hunch, he rode down toward the east, and sure enough, there was the man walking along the highway. The officer stopped and arrested him. I thought my little 105 pound wife did a wise thing. The reason they did not call for help, was that there was no phone at the church, and the phone at the pastorium had been cut off. That was before cell phones.

While I was still driving the truck, I was told I was required to attend in-service training class taught by the institution psychologist. I had rather be whipped with a croaker sack full of salt water catfish than take these classes. But, I'm sure someone got some benefit out of it. I was late going to class at night, so the only seat left was on the front row. The teacher (psychologist) was really fired up teaching the class. The subject was, "Proper enthusiasm on the job". He said that a person must have the proper amount of ambition. The example he used was a truck driver. He said, "A truck driver does not have a lot of intelligence or ambition, just watching the road, and mashing the brake when told to by the red-light." He just kept on belittling the dumb old truckers. The class started laughing. He thought he had said something funny, and kept on with it. Finally he stopped and asked, "What is so funny?" Someone said, "Mr. Gilley, sitting right there in front of you is a truck driver." He looked at me. I crossed my eyes, and stuck my tongue out at him. He hushed up about us low class people.

While writing about night classes, there was one that I remember. It was one that my wife needed also since she worked at purchasing at the Florida State Hospital. The class was on first aid. I remember it well. The first thing we learned was how to stop bleeding by using pressure bandages. We also learned if a limb, arm or leg, has a bleeding laceration, you should elevate it to stop bleeding. When my wife and I were getting ready for bed that night, I pulled my shoes off, and undressed to get a shower. Going into the bathroom, I had on nothing but my shorts. I have always been like the woods a fire moving around the house. When I turned into the doorway to the bathroom, I didn't turn fast enough, and kicked the sharp edge of the facing. The third toe on my right foot hit the facing so hard, it split my toe nail. The pain was unbearable. If you have never kicked a bed leg, or a door facing, you cannot appreciate what I am about to say. I fell down in the hallway groaning. My wife came out to see what all the fuss was about. She saw me wallowing around like a beached porpoise and it struck her funny. When she gets struck funny, you just as well let her get over it. I decided I would really put on a joke for her. I yelled, "It is bleeding." and it was. It was just a drop of blood. I yelled, "Apply a pressure bandage, but first let me elevate it." I rolled over and put my injured foot in the telephone chair. My poor sympathetic wife had tears in her eyes, not from crying or sympathy though, but from horse laughing. I then yelled, "Put a tourniquet on it to stop it from bleeding!" It must have taken 30 minutes for this to transpire. When my wife gets depressed now, all I have to do to make her laugh, is to mention the split toe and tourniquet and she starts laughing.

Yesterday I needed to find out a date for this book. I went to my dresser drawer where I have my ACI personnel file which I put there 8 years ago last week, and pulled out the old folder. It has all my leave slips, vacation and sick time. All my promotions, and applications for promotions, and some things I had forgotten all about. I grinned when I saw them. There were 13 certificates of appreciation, and personal letters of appreciation, 11 certificates of achievements. I guess that ain't too bad for 38 years: 22 atta boys. I didn't average one a year, but I wasn't working for those things. It made me feel good when my wife read them to me. You see, I am legally blind, and cannot read a thing since 1998. I can't complain though, because I've had macular degeneration since I was 38 years old. The Dr. told me I would have to retire from office work by the time I was 50, but I worked until I was 65, lacking two days.

ACI was approved to receive surplus property from the federal government. For some reason, Eglin Air Force Base had a semi-truck load of household furniture: beds, dressers, chest of drawers, chairs, tables, etc. They brought it into our institution, and stored the whole lot in the basement of one of the inmate dormitories. I was equipment manager at the time. They turned it over to me to inventory and make suggestions about what to do with it. At that time, we only had three bachelor quarters, and the superintendent's house that were furnished. We really had no need for this equipment. After I inventoried it, and found no need for any of the stuff, I recommended that it be included with the used surplus of the institution, and an auction be held for state employees to get rid of it. When I gave my suggestion to the business manager, he had to get it approved by the superintendent. He told me to give him a plan as to when it would be held, the place, and who the auctioneer would be. Well, the time I decided would be at 5:30 pm, giving morning shift people 30 minutes after their shift. The place would be right where it was, because I wasn't about to move all that stuff. The plan was for the buyer to pay cash at the time of the auction, and be prepared to move the stuff that day. I would do something I had never done: auctioneer. I had been to plenty of auctions. I had a ball. I knew almost everyone there. I had gone down and tried to sort out the pieces. The hard part was the beds. When I got down to the last beds, no foot boards or head boards matched. So, I just left all the odd pieces in a pile back in a corner.

The business office was in charge of numbering the pieces, and collecting the money from successful bidders. There were some beautiful air force platters made of heavy china. Everybody wanted one of them. I just put a price of $1.00 on them. Sold almost all

100 of them. It was summertime, and no air conditioning in the basement. Man, were we sweating, especially me. But, everybody was in the bidding mood. I remember I made a rule, no bid less than a dollar would be accepted. So, an increase of 25 cents, or less than a dollar would not be accepted. One pretty, nice round dining room oak table was quite popular. I remember it started out with a $5.00 bid. It worked up to $15.00, and everyone except two men quit bidding. It was back and forth with no hesitation until it got to $27.00. One of the men said, "Do you really want that table friend?" His friend replied, "I sure do." The first man said, "Well, then you won't mind bidding for it. $35.00" The second man failed to bid, and I took the $35.00 bid. Another piece that was popular was a fold up or down stove top. It was removed from the Superintendent's house. I told the bidders that it was just recently removed from his kitchen and replaced with a regular stove. Bidding started with several people participating. I knew several of them wanted it just because it belonged to the boss. Two men ran the price up to $30.00. I felt guilty and confessed that both of the electric eyes on the stove were burned out. I knew there was no love between the bidders. One said, "I don't care. I can replace them. I want it for my camper." The other bidder said, "I want it for my church. $35.00." The other said, "Can't go against the Lord." By this time, we came to the beds. Good luck! I sold everyone that I had set aside as complete. When I got to this point, I said, "That's all folks." Someone said, "Not yet." He had gone down to the odd pieces, got a head board with non matching foot board, two different rails, and said, "Bid this one." I said, "Bids will open at $5.00. Do I hear a bid?" The man who dug it out said, "$5.00". I said, "Sold to the gentleman." I stopped, held my clipboard loosely in my left hand, and turned to speak with some people who were there gathering up their loot, and here came another bed being drug up by a matchmaker of odds and ends. Same procedure! That went on until almost all the beds were gone. All bid $5.00, and I would say, "Sold to the gentleman." I looked back in the pile, and saw my good friend, the purchasing agent. I went over to another good friend, and said, "When the purchasing agent brings his bed up and says $5.00, you say I bid $15.00." I told another man to bid $25.00 when that man

said 15. Well, here came the purchasing agent with his bed. When I asked him what he bid, he said, "$5.00". Then the first man said, "I bid $15." The second man said, "I bid $25." The purchasing agent was already hot and mad because his wife was making him pick through that pile of junk. He dropped the bed and said, "You bastards, that's my bed!" and he started out of the basement mad as a wet hen. I took after him, and caught him at the door. I said, "You didn't hear what I said. I said, sold to the handsome man for $5.00" He stopped and looked at me for a long time. I said, "I'll help you carry it out." As we went out, he was carrying the two rails, and I was carrying the headboard under one arm, and the foot board under the other arm. He said, "Gilley, you are a true friend, but I don't know about those other two that tried to take my bed." I never told him that I had set the other men up. I don't know whether anyone else did or not. I never heard it mentioned again. I considered that the cruelest joke that I ever did. That day I made a lot of friends, made $598.00 for the revolving fund, and also got the basement cleaned out completely.

I don't believe you could get away with that kind of business now. I know I sure am glad I am retired, and out of the mess.

It took me two years to gear my work habits down to snail's pace to fit the state's work pace. I had been with office work for the railroad for 9 years, and it is "hump and get it". If you don't get your work done in 8 hours on the railroad, it is left for the next shift to do. You don't leave any of your work for the next shift without a perfect reason. Maybe the telegraph lines were down, or a train wreck had closed down a track or some such thing. With ACI, I would send a survey report to a department head to sign, and I expected it to be back within two days. Sometimes it took 30 to 40 days. My complaining or pleading made no difference. After two years of this, I mentioned it to the superintendent. He said, "Mr. Gilley, this is not the railroad. We have no train to catch. If you don't get it done, there is always tomorrow. This place is here because of inmates, and they have nothing but time. Slow down, and get in step with everyone else." I tried, but I never did get tolerant of dragging my feet, or procrastination.

There is one thing that I have learned though, and that is to laugh in silence and without expression. When you are working inmates in an office setting, young men will sometimes say or do funny things, don't laugh out loud or express any humor on your face. If you do, the inmates will do anything to make you laugh because they will get on your good side, and become a pest and make your life miserable.

There is one time that I can recall with vivid memory. In the early days of my employment with the State, they fed us three meals a day. One morning at breakfast the purchasing agent and I were at the same table with four others at a six-man table. The purchasing agent hit his spoon on the table with his elbow knocking it into the floor. An inmate that was the best helper in the dining room that we ever had . He was well kept, had good manners, and was disciplined. He was standing watching us eat, ready to do anything for our needs. As soon as the spoon hit the floor, he jumped and grabbed it, rubbed it on his pants leg, and put it right back where it was. I was looking straight at him with my elbow propped on the table, with my chin in my left hand because had finished my meal . I was finishing drinking my coffee, waiting on the work whistle. The purchasing agent was still eating when the inmate replaced the spoon back on the table.

The purchasing agent saw him clean it on his pants. He just rolled his head and looked at the inmate with disdain out of the corner of his eyes. The inmate was looking straight at me. I did not change my expression on my face although I was laughing like crazy inside. I think maybe my eyes gave me away. The inmate gave a sly, half-grin, and before the purchasing agent could remark at all, he reached and picked up the spoon. When he left the purchasing agent looked at me, and with his eyes asked me, did you see that? I slightly nodded my head. That was the first time that I remember holding in a laugh when I wanted to laugh out loud. What I did was tell my wife and daughter after work and after supper. Then I would really laugh about it with them.

When the business office was in the warehouse, there was an inmate working there when I came. I didn't know any of their names, but their shirts had a strip of cloth sewed over the pocket, and their names were stenciled on the cloth. The inmate that was in the office was named John, and I heard an inmate call him "Joanie". I didn't ask why, but from his strutting walk, and his way of talking, I knew why, he was homosexual. "Sweet Boy" they called him. His desk was straight across the office from my desk. It was a big open office with nine desks in one room. I was at my desk, and I heard someone walking, dragging their shoe soles on the concrete floor. I just moved my eyes, not my head, and saw John going toward the purchasing agent's desk. The inmate walked around behind the desk where the purchasing agent was sitting. The inmate had a piece of paper in his hand, and he went and stood real close to the purchasing agent, and called him by name. The purchasing agent looked up and said, "Boy, get on the other side of my desk." Needless to say, he moved, and never tried that again. I kept my eyes on this man the rest of the time that he spent with us.

The purchasing agent was in the record room, which was in the warehouse just to the right as you go into the warehouse from the office. It was the policy to lock up the record room when we went to lunch. The walls and door to the record room were made of 3-inch slats, with a 3-inch space between slats. A padlock was used to secure the door at noon. The lock was left open, unlocked, hanging in the hasp. On this day, the purchasing agent had Joanie with him in the record room looking for an old purchase order. When it came time for lunch, all the inmates were just finishing unloading a truck at the back door of the warehouse, and they were told to go line up for count in the office. When they came by the record room, an inmate just put the lock in the hasp with the door shut and locked it. When we counted the inmates, we were one short. Someone asked where was Joanie? About that time I heard the purchasing agent yelling bloody murder in four letter words. They had locked the purchasing agent in the record room with Joanie! When the purchasing agent got out he thought an officer did it on purpose, but one of our best inmates said, "I did it, Sir, I didn't know there was anyone in there." The purchasing agent said, "There is a new rule, starting now. No one locks a door without yelling, is there anyone in there?" One more thing about this inmate, when his time was up, the night before he was to leave, he intentionally disobeyed a direct order to get the classification people to take away his gain time, and they did, and he stayed 3 more months until his full expiration date arrived. He loved it at A. C. I. One officer said, "I don't understand it." I said, "Well, it would be like you being locked up with 500 pretty women!" "Oh yeah!" he said.

In the early 70's I was crossing from one side of the administration building to another, and I saw the horticulture supervisor standing at the top of the stairs looking out through the big glass windows toward highway 90. I looked out that way and saw 18 men along the road that leads out to the highway, and I noticed something different. Every man along the road had in his hand what we lovingly call a "yo-yo". They are really a grass sling. I knew the department had plenty of lawn mowers and push type mowers. I asked, "What is happening, sir?" He told me, "While I was waiting for the work whistle to blow, I went exploring behind the horticulture shack and found a gallon jug full of "buck". I just left it where it was and waited on my crew to show up. When they showed up, I told them that I was going to be easy on them for making "buck", if they brought the gallon jug, and put it in the office while I was in the front office picking up the mail. You can't drink it anyway, because I peed in it. Well, I came up here, and when I returned to the shack, there in the middle of my office, were 5 gallons of "buck". They didn't know which jug I had found, so they had to turn them all in. Since I didn't know who was guilty of "buck" making, I decided the whole department needed disciplining. So, all of them are getting some old fashioned disciplining. Those "yo-yos" will get their attention." Maybe I should explain what "buck" is. Home-brew is another name for the nasty stuff. Inmates will make it from just about anything. Blackberries were the fruit those guys used. They just put them in a container with no top, and put some sugar and water on them, and if available, yeast will speed up the fermenting process. A few weeks will give you enough alcohol to curl your hair.

Anytime you lock young men up, they will find things with which to entertain themselves, such as gambling. The State takes all the inmates' money to keep them from gambling, as well as not being able to purchase contraband. We had a problem with gambling for cigarettes. Some of the slick inmates would have 8 to 10 cartons at one time in their foot lockers. They had not made any purchase from the canteen. The only place they could get them was illegal activities. So, we restricted the inmates from having more than two packs of cigarettes at any given time. Then, they started gambling for tennis shoes. One man had ten pair of tennis shoes. You really have to be on your toes to stay ahead of those guys.

Since I started writing this book, it seems that something wild or exciting happened every day. Then I remember that I'm covering 38 years, and that is a lifetime for some people. The incident that brought this line of thinking about happened at night. When I went to work the next day, I noticed some people gathered on the lawn of the administration building in which my office was located. I walked over to the people and exclaimed, "Good grief!" There in the front of the building just short of the access road was a sink hole: 14 feet in circumference, and 12 feet deep. As I looked down into this monstrous hole, I became uneasy being so close, and thinking the walls could collapse and swallow me up too. Wheels began to turn in my little ole' brain. I need to get in touch with the construction office in Tallahassee. I later wondered why I called the construction department. I guess it was because I knew one of the engineers really well, and I knew that if this was not his problem, he would direct me to the right place. He knew what to do because in south Florida this happens all the time. He said we need to get to work real soon and get the loose dirt out of the hole all the way down to the lime rock if possible, and if not, as deep as our drag line could reach. Then pack what is left and cover the bottom of the hole with bags of cement, bag and all. They told me not to let anyone get down into the hole unless they were in a drag line bucket. It was too dangerous. I called our construction department and told them to bring our drag line and several dump trucks to have the dirt hauled off that we dug out of the hole, and dump it someplace until we could plug the hole. The supervisor said, "No problem." We worked until 3 pm digging out loose dirt, and then got one of the crew to go down in the bucket of the drag line, and take a ten foot piece of reinforcing rod and probe for the lime rock. There was no lime rock within reach. So, I told them to start packing the loose dirt in the bottom with the bucket. The hole now was 20 feet deep. The reason I know the size of the hole is because I was told to keep records by the Tallahassee office. I then sent a correctional officer to the cement shack to bring 20 bags of concrete. I had the inmates to drop the bags flat, and try to cover the bottom of the hole completely with the bags of concrete. Looked good. Then, we reversed the activities, hauled all the loose dirt back into the hole. Finished the job by 5 pm. What a day! The local newspaper found out about it, and came and took pictures. We made the front page. The next day, I called Tallahassee back and reported job complete except no sod had been put back on top of the refilled hole. My friend told me he had already made arrangements for a well-drilling outfit to come over and drill a hole through the pavement in the street to determine the size of the cavity. Since the sump hole was right next to the street and the parking lot, they didn't want to hear of half of the employees at ACI coming out to go home after work and finding their vehicles down in a hole. It took two days for the well digging rig to come. They had no trouble finding the hole. It was a 6 inch hole that they drilled in the road. They hit open space at 30 feet. When they were finished, they were released and sent home. Then the next day, we had 3 concrete companies to start hauling concrete to fill the hole. They made a chute to direct the Redimix into the hole. Although it has been almost 15 years, I well remember, it took 19 truckloads, 180 cubic yards of Redimix to fill the cavity below the road.

I had never heard of the Panhandle of Florida having sink holes. When I told our beef herd manager this, he said, "Why just last year I went missing a cow and a calf. I went looking for them and heard the cow bawling and went to her. I found her standing at the edge of a sink hole looking down at her calf standing on the bottom. We managed to get the calf out with webbing and ropes." I said, "Did you fill the hole in?" "No," he said, "Just put barbed wire fence around it. You can go down to the south pasture and see it if you want to." I planned to go see it, but I never did, probably won't now.

In November 1968 the new administration building was completed and the superintendent, assistant superintendent, business manager, classification personnel, and staff dining plus the security captain all moved into the space. It was such an improvement over the old offices in which they were located. My office was in the far corner toward the west. I liked my new office space. It was not private. It was a large room with six desks in it for three officers and three inmates. I liked my job too. The only deadline I had was July 1 of each year, which was when I had to have all my inventorying done by the fiscal year's end. Both warehouse stores and capital outlay. I could do it anytime during the year. I always started in January so I wouldn't be rushed. The rest of the time I learned purchasing and helping out anywhere I was needed. I kept the new purchasing contracts filed and read each one. I knew them better than the purchasing agent. I was still the equipment manager with the title of accountant clerk. When the purchasing agent was off duty for any reason, I worked his job and did the purchasing for him. I really worked hard to please the department heads on a timely basis. They got to the point of waiting on the purchasing agent to be off so I could purchase for them. They nor I ever told the purchasing agent about this. It's O.K. to say it now because he has been dead for five years.

I was sure that I would get the job of purchasing when the purchasing agent was made industries manager. I started not to even apply for the job, but the personnel officer said he needed an application for the files. I got the job in 1971, and the purchasing agent just left out the day he was promoted, and never looked back. He said, "I know you know the job as good as I do. You don't need me to teach you anything, do you?" I said, "Good bye," and never needed to ask him a single question. His office was just across the hall, which made me feel good, even though I never needed him.

Things began to grow by leaps and bounds. Federal grants, seven in all, new programs, and new industries which totaled 13. But, as things grew, I grew with them. I had no problem with being overworked. But then it happened, the department grew so big, they split it into five regions. Ours was region one which was the panhandle of Florida from Tallahassee west, including Tallahassee. When it was determined that it would happen for sure, the director came to ACI to tell us it was final. When he got through telling about personnel, security, finance, administration and all the rest, he asked for any questions. I stood up and asked who was going to do the purchasing for the region. He said Tallahassee would retain that job. I said, "I don't believe that any more than I believe I can jump over this building backwards. You better make provisions to have purchasing done on the regional level." He politely told me it would not happen.

The split took place. The regional staff took over one wing of the administration building at ACI just next door, around the corner from me. They rocked along for about three months. Then one day a girl from the regional office came into my office and said, The region was meeting in the conference room next door, and the assistant director wanted me to be in the meeting. I knew what was coming. When I got settled in at the big meeting, the assistant director who was a friend of mine, softly said, "Mr. Gilley, we are here to discuss purchasing for the Region 1." He paused for a long time, then he said, "It looks like you will be doing the purchasing for us." I asked, "For the same money?" His reply was a weak, "Yes." I asked, "with the same help?" His reply was the same as before, "Yes." My reply to that was, "The hell you say." I got up and walked out. When I first went in, I asked where the director was. The assistant director said he was needed somewhere else. I went back to my office and thought about what I had said and done. Then I went to my superintendent and told him what I had done. He and I were good buddies, hunting doves and playing dominoes together. He called me "Gil" and I called him "Chief". When I told him that I worked for him and not the region, he said, "I'll back you all the way, Gil. You do work for me and they ain't asked me nothing about this. If you don't want to work for them, I'll understand, and it won't hurt my feelings. But, you think about it, and if you decide what it will take for you to take on the extra work, I'll back you."

I went over to the assistant director's office and apologized to him for the things I said. I told him the thing I was sorry for was that the director was not man enough to face me after I told him, and the director of prisons that purchasing in Tallahassee would not work. He said, "I know, Cliff, how you feel. You feel like someone is trying to dump on you." I told him also to tell the big man that he wouldn't face me today, but he'll have to face me before it's over. You tell him not to send you, or I'll walk out again. I want him to look me in the eye and say, "You were right."

Well, the next day the next day the superintendent called me into his office, and there sat the director. I stepped inside the door and glared one of my meanest Gilley glares at him, waiting for him to say something. The director said, "I understand you refuse to purchase for Region one." I said, "I work for this man, and he hasn't told me to purchase for you." The superintendent said, "And I'm not going to tell you that, Gil. That is your choice." The thought came into my mind that I have never in my life had a man with the authority that the director had, in such a position. There was no one in the region that knew anything about the purchasing rules, regulations, and most importantly, the laws. If you break the laws of purchasing, it's just like breaking any other law, because you can go to jail, and ignorance is no excuse, because, every state prison has a copy of the statutes. I thought, "I've got this man between a rock and a hard place." His boss was the one that decided not to purchase on the regional level. I said, "I'll purchase for you under three conditions: first, you admit that I was right. He said, "You got it." Second, that I be permitted to move into the back of the building into the office vacated by the captain when he moved into the multi treatment building, and take the girl secretary with me that I am now sharing with the business manager. Third, I get promoted to purchasing agent III with a 10% increase in pay. He said, "It's agreed." Then he asked how making more money would make me able to do more work. I said, "If I'm a purchasing agent III, I will be able to close my door to everyone, and they can only see me by appointment, and thus I'll have time to apply to my work load. The next morning, there was a work squad knocking at my door ready to move me to my new location. Well, I said, that was soon enough, now let me see how fast they will get my raise through. Seems that legislators and budget committee had to approve that, but it came in. Well, things worked pretty well, except a few things had to be worked out.

Some of the road camp captains had been doing their own purchasing of some items, and they did not want to stop. I recalled that we were to ship food stuff from our warehouse, and our meat processing plant twice a month. One day I received a phone call from our meat truck driver saying that the captain at one of our road camps was refusing the hamburger meat that he had on the truck. I said, "That's fine now. You set it aside in your freezer on the truck and bring it back to us. Keep it frozen, and let me know when you get back. If you don't get back before night, let your freezer run all night. Don't let that meat thaw."

The next morning the driver called me, and I went to the warehouse and got the meat. I told the meat cutting supervisor to cut me five pounds off the block of meat and send the rest of it to the kitchen. Tell our chief cook to cook the meat and call me with the test results. I took the five pound block to the staff dining kitchen, and told the cook to make as many hamburgers as she could from that meat. Before I gave her the meat, I took a half-pound off and had it sent to the Florida food testing lab for results for human consumption. I told the regional director I wanted him to eat a hamburger that we were trying for taste tests. He passed it with flying colors, and so did the inmate kitchen. The next morning, I got the test from the testing lab in Tallahassee, and it read, "Good for human consumption." Now, I had what I wanted. I called the captain that had refused the meat, and told him, "The meat that you refused has been eaten by the director and his staff. The inmate population at ACI, and the testing lab at Tallahassee states it is good for human consumption. Now, I know you have been ordering your meat from Swift and Co. and that they have been giving you a turkey personally at Thanksgiving, and a ham at Christmas. I know you want to keep buying from them, but let me tell you the only way you can continue to purchase from them is for you to use your own money and buy for yourself. Now, I don't want to make you receive meat if it is not good, but your refusing all that is sent to you, will not result in my allowing you to do my job for me. I promise you, if you become a problem to me, I will get your job". Then I asked, "Any questions?" "No sir," he said. I said, "You understand and will comply?" "Yes sir," he said. I said, "Thank you, captain, and I hope you are not going to let this keep us from being the best of friends." "No sir," he said. He didn't, and as long as I worked with him, he was the nicest non-complaining captain that I worked with.

One morning when I got to work, the Lieutenant that was on duty on Saturday morning came to me and handed me a 5"X7" piece of green paper. I asked, "What is this?" He said, "It is a receipt for a confiscated flash note. The federal investigator took it off your desk while he was here Saturday." I asked, "What was he doing in my office?" He replied, "I let him in to investigate an inmate, and he found the paper on your desk. He said it was illegal and confiscated it, and told me to give you this note. I said, "That office is full of secret, sealed bids, and are not open to the public. The flash note he called it, was a religious tract. It was the half size of a twenty dollar bill on one side, it looked like a folded twenty dollar bill, and on the other side, there were scripture references. My older sister is very religious, and is married to a Baptist preacher. She gave me five of these tracts for witnessing purposes. They were important to me since my sister gave them to me. I don't get to see her very often because she lives in Tennessee."

It made me so angry, I told that lieutenant, that it was a stupid thing he did letting that man in my office, and I was going to see if I could get his job for it. You can tell your federal friend he is in the same boat. You had no business opening a purchasing office to anyone, even yourself. I am going to get in touch with my senator and representative to see if I can get the federal man's job also. If they don't get him fired, I'm going to bring suit against him for taking anything without a search warrant. He went straight and called the federal man I know, because he called me and tried to scare me into dropping the case by telling me that I could be fired and jailed if it were pushed. I told him that I had already contacted a big important lawyer in Tallahassee, and he said he would take the case for no fee, just to get the chance to go to court, and see a federal man like that squirm. I also told him that his threat to get me to drop the case would be mentioned in the lawsuit. Before I hung up on him, I said, "I'll see you in court." It was true about the lawyer. I had been to Greensboro the night before, and had shown the receipt for the flash note to a lawyer and told him it was made by the Southern Baptist Convention. He laughed, and said he would take the case at no cost. He was the guest speaker at a Baptist church meeting when I saw him. I had every intention of suing the guy for anything I could think of. The Lieutenant said the hardest thing he ever had to do was give me that receipt. I knew you would be fit to be tied. I said, "Why didn't you tell him to use the conference room next door?" "Well," he said, "Your office is so much nicer than the conference room. You have all those beautiful plants, and your beautiful wood carvings. I had no idea that he would make a fool of himself and me too.

Well, I had work to do the rest of the day, so I went on about my business. The next day the superintendent called me at 10:00 am and said, "Gil, we are having a dove shoot down south of Sneads at a certain field tomorrow afternoon. We want you to come." I said, "Thanks Chief, I'll be there." Then he said, "Oh, by the way, I want a favor from you." I had no idea what he was about to say. He said, "I want you to drop the matter between you and the Federal Inspector." I paused before answering, wondering how in the world did he get into it. He then said, "This is a friend of mine." I said, "O.K. Chief, but keep him away from me and my stuff." "Will do," he said. The next afternoon I went down to the appointed field, and got right in the middle of the field. That is the best place to shoot that field. I had been there many times before. About 3:00 the birds started to fly. They came in from every direction. When they passed over the fence rows, they would drop down in the middle of the field. There was a hunter about 40 yards away in the top fence row of the field. He must have yelled, "Cliff, coming in from the north" 25 times or more. I got my limit of 12 in about an hour and left, which was the wise thing to do because the game warden hears of these shoots and comes hunting for poachers. I didn't want to be arrested for a few tiny little ole birds. I left the field then, and started home . When I got to the fence where my car was, I saw a man who worked on our farm at the West Unit. I asked him, "Who was that guy up there that kept hollering, 'Cliff, coming in from the north'?" He said, "Oh you know him, Mr. Gilley, that is the federal investigator down here on a case, and doing some hunting while he's here. He is a friend of the superintendent." To myself I said, "I'm glad I didn't know it was him, or I might have sprayed him with bird shot a few times."

When the administration building was built, they left a spot in the center of the building that was 40' X 40' that was just grass and right in the center was a small flower bed with a big century plant. That thing was huge. As the years passed, I researched the thing, and found out the reason it was called a century plant was because it lives for 100 years, then blooms and dies. I found out that this plant was no older than 40 years old. When this plant bloomed and died, the institution was only 40 years old. One day I noticed a big round stalk coming up in the middle of the plant about 2" in diameter. It started to grow in April, by August it was 16 feet tall with branches growing straight out for 2 or 3 feet, and turning straight up for 2 or 3 feet, then a bunch of little pods with blooms on the sides of them came on the ends of the branches. I looked at it the first thing each day. It was right in front of my office door. I had never seen such a thing as that. The local newspaper came and took pictures and wrote an article about it.

Seems like we were always getting in the paper for something, but it was usually for good that we did. We did not air our dirty laundry in public places.

Shortly after the century plant died, I was made chairman of the beautification committee. Sounds strange for a prison to have such a committee. I love flowers and have hundreds in my double lot yard at home. They thought I would be good for the committee. I took my job seriously. In fact, on highway 90 west of the Apalachicola River, you will find a beautiful entrance built of white brick which leads to the parking lot in front of the administration building at ACI. It is 1300 feet from the parking lot to the highway. I know for I stepped it off for crepe myrtle trees every 15 feet, and a water line with a hose faucet every 100 feet. I turned the digging the ditches over to the disciplinary squad, knowing it would keep them busy for several days because there were water lines on both sides of the road, that was 2600 feet of ditches to dig with pick and shovel. But, someone thought differently, because, by the time I got my office work done, and went out to the project site, they were halfway finished digging ditches on one side of the road to the highway. The squad leader went to the construction supervisor, and got him to go to Marianna to rent a ditch witch, a gasoline powered ditch digger. They finished all of that project in one day. When you pass the entrance of the institution, you will be able to enjoy the beautification committee's work. The white and pink crepe myrtle trees are a sight to see, and the brick work too. I was responsible for that. I drew the blue print, ordered the brick, rented an underground drill and operator, and drilled under highway 90. Our electricians ran the electricity to the entrance under the highway. It took some "finagling" to get the brick laid. There was a good brick laying inmate at the West Unit, but he was classified "maximum security" with a 25 years to life for murder. I went to bat with classification and the superintendent for the man. He had pulled 8 years of his sentence and had a good record the whole time. The supervisor of the brick laying squad wanted this man to do the laying of the brick. The officer had been shot in the right arm, and had no use of it, so he could not show a man how it should be done, although he had the knowledge. I finally called the powers to be and asked them to permit the man to go to medium security, which meant that the inmate could not be left alone. He was not under the gun, though.

We wanted the letters spelling Apalachee Correctional Institution on one side of the entrance, and Department of Corrections on the other side. I had the sheet metal shop to make these letters with a strap to be laid in with the brick so anyone trying to remove the lettering would have to tear the wall down because they are attached. Every time I drive by there, and see the flowers and the light at night with the sprinklers going in dry weather, I think of all the trouble I went to accomplish that site. As long as I worked there, they called that entrance, "Gilley's gate." I don't know, after 8 years, if there is anyone there that remembers it now, but I surely do.

I enjoyed working on the committee because anything we wanted to do, the regional director was in favor. I had the inside garden of the administration building totally changed. For the center of the area, I put a fountain that I purchased from a man who makes concrete tables, seats, and all manners of what-knots, sidewalks and benches. This made a very attractive place for visitors of the inmates to visit. The fountain caused some dissension because it had a nude woman on the top of it, but before long, no one even mentioned it.

One thing worth mentioning was, several years ago, we had a cold winter, and the steam pipes from the boiler room and the green house burst, and every plant that was in the green house at the time froze, and was lost. We had a special fund at that time called the green house fund. Certain garden clubs used this as a project to make contributions to this fund, and we used it to buy flowers, trees, and beautification items for the compound where inmates could enjoy them. Our superintendent received a letter from the Northwest Florida Garden Club requesting someone from ACI come and speak to their garden club's annual meeting. The superintendent flagged the letter to me and asked me to take care of it. When the day arrived for the meeting, I just closed the purchasing office, took my secretary along to make notes, and do what good secretaries do. The meeting house was full. The people had been meeting all day, and my time to speak was at 2 pm. I arrived at 1:45 pm and walked into a loud clapping of hands, and a welcome reserved for celebrities. My secretary leaned over to me and asked, "Are you sure we're at the right place?" We found a place to sit under the stair case, and in just a few minutes it was my turn to speak. When I got up to speak, I was told that I had three minutes to speak. The first thing I said was, "Our green house contents were lost during the cold weather, and the steam lines burst. Then I felt someone tugging at my coat tail. I said, "That's the shortest three minutes I ever saw." The lady said, "Your time is not up, I just wanted to tell you we are taking up a collection for your green house fund." I said, "I did not come here to beg for money." By that time, they had a shoe box going around. When it got around, I was finished with my three minute speech. They gave me the box of money. I gave it to my secretary and told her to count it and give the ladies a receipt. There was a total of $82.35. I thanked them and they had convinced me and my secretary that we should hit the road doing speeches for $82.35 per three minutes. If we did this we could retire in a week.

It was about the time in my career that the Division of Purchasing began holding state wide purchasing workshops once a year lasting for a week. The Department of Corrections decided we should be doing the same thing, and we did. When we had our purchasing meeting, we would invite the Division of Purchasing to come and help with learning and teaching purchasing procedures. Our Department of Corrections' Purchasing Director decided it would be a good thing to do a skit showing how to conduct a bid opening in the correct and incorrect ways. He got three other purchasing agents and me to put on a skit, and we had fun with it.

Two months later, the big purchasing agency for the whole state called the Division of Corrections Purchasing and requested that the same group come and put the skit on for them at their annual meeting. That was the last time that I remember having stage fright. These people were our bosses, and I was afraid of offending some of them, but we did the skit anyway. I played a drunk bidder. I flirted with the secretary, and tried to bribe the purchasing agent who was opening the bid. I came in late, I failed to sign my bid, and wanted to sign it after the bids were all opened. I failed to put the figure I was bidding, and wanted to fill it in after the bidding was over. I signed my name in pencil instead of ink. I offered the purchasing agent a drink of my booze. I put my feet on the desk, and had some FSU football tickets which I offered to the purchasing agent. The people all got a big laugh over the wrong way to have a bid opening skit. I was looking through my old files, and found a letter of appreciation from the Director of the Division of Purchasing for this activity.

I worked real close with the industries program for years until they turned it over to a private organization. We had the only brick plant in the State of Florida. We could not make a #1 brick, but made a pretty good #2 brick. Every once in a while, we would get a brick that was not the same thickness on both ends, but all the buildings at ACI were made out of our bricks. In the late 1980s the demand for brick fell through the floor because no one wanted them. Brick masons became fewer and fewer. The cost to lay them skyrocketed, and concrete block took over the market. So, we closed down the plant. My business manager and I managed to sell the plant to a company in North Carolina. It was nice to know that the old brick plant was still going to be used.

The lot where the brick plant was located, was used for gathering scrap metal. It fell my lot to sell the scrap metal. I knew nothing about scrap metal, and even less about scrap dealers. I didn't even try to estimate the amount of metal to each lot of copper, iron, steel, aluminum, and brass. I just advertised them by lots. By the time I had done this for five years, I got the hang of it. There was a pair of scales at the Florida State Hospital, and we had a pair of scales at the poultry department. I would make the empty truck weigh, and get a weight ticket, then when it was loaded, I would make them weigh again, and they would have to pay with cash per pound, before they left town. I learned that trick the first year when a metal company waited six months and fifteen phone calls before paying their debt. The scrap dealers loved to come to ACI because we had some good scrap metal. I remember there was a man that bought copper from the local people, took his pickup and hauled it to Dothan, AL, and got a few cents per pound more for it there to make himself some spending money. He was crippled, and could hardly walk, but he did O.K. He was high bidder on the copper one year. We had a lot of small pieces, such as pipe fitting, and short pieces of wire. Somewhere we had come by a copper steam kettle that held 50 gallons. As we got small pieces of copper, we just threw them into the copper kettle. It took a year to fill the kettle full of small pieces of copper. When my friend came to pickup his copper, he weighed empty, and loaded up. Our inmates loaded the copper for him. I asked him if he wanted us to dump the copper into his truck bed so he could see what he was getting. He said, "Oh, no, I'd never get it all picked up. Just leave it sitting up." He left and weighed and paid me cash. I went back to the institution, gave the cash to the industries accountant, and thought the deal was closed. The next day the crippled man came to my office with a sad story. He said when he got to the metal company to sell his copper, they turned the kettle over, and it had 100 pounds of water in it from the rain. He showed me his weight ticket the dealer had given him, and sure enough, it was 100 pounds lighter than the ticket I had. He said, "I lost all my profit." I told him not to worry, he had more copper to pickup, and when he picked up another truck load, and weighed out, I reduced the poundage by 100 pounds. I made a friend for life. He assured me he would never buy a lot in a poke again.

When the state started paying for officers' uniforms, the department of general services, Division of Purchasing, entered into a contract with a clothing manufacturing company to furnish uniforms for the whole prison system. It worked really well. All I had to do was use the commodity number and cut a purchase order for the size and number of shirts or pants, and they shipped them to us. The security department kept them where inmates could not get to them, so they could not steal them, and just walk out pretending to be an officer.

One day I got an order for three pair of pants 54" in the waist. When the company got my purchase order, they called me and said they could not furnish the pants in the material that the contract called for because it was not wide enough. They could furnish them in a different material with a slight change of color, a lighter brown. I agreed to take the pants in a lighter color. When the pants came in, the officer brought them to my office and gave them to me and said that they were the wrong color, and he was not going to wear them. "Well," I said, "They will be right here, because no one else in the system wears that size, and they are not returnable." He said, "This pair that I have on is the only pair that I have, and I'm washing them every night so I'll have clean pants to wear every day." I said, "Well, I have done all I can do legally, and I darn sure ain't going to do anything illegal for someone as picky as you." Then, I added, "But, if you can find someone that will make pants to suit you, you can pay for them with your money, and I'll approve them for you to wear." I thought it was all over, and he would continue to wear the same pair of pants, but he decided he would go over my head, and went to the assistant superintendent and told him his sad story. The assistant superintendent told him the pants are O.K. to wear. One color shade different would not matter. He felt, I'm sure, that the inmates would notice it, and give him all kinds of problems. The assistant superintendent told him, "If I were you, I would keep them, and use them for shelter halves." Boy oh boy, those two guys were pretty close pals, but not after that episode. The assistant superintendent came to my office just down the hall and told me what he had done. He was quite a big man himself, and I figured he felt by his being large too, he could joke about it, but not so.

The assistant superintendent and I met in Hardee's just this week, and I told him about writing this book, and asked him if I could put this story in my book, and he laughed and said, "By all means". In fact, he was tickled to death when someone drew his picture running with a telephone pole over his shoulder. The caption of this cartoon was that he was going to participate in the Olympics as a pole vaulter.

I kept those three pair of size 54 pants in my file cabinet for three years wondering what to do with them. One day the chief cook came into my office with a request for two pair of size 54 security uniform pants. The chief cook was one of my best pals. I looked at him, smiling from ear to ear. He said, "I know what you are thinking." I asked, "What am I thinking?" He came back with, "I didn't know you had a blimp working for you." "Oh no. I got you that time. I was thinking, does he think this is Sears and Roebuck" he's shopping in?" I got up from my desk, walked to the file cabinet, and said, "Boy, do I have a deal for you. Buy two, get one free." I pulled out the drawer, took out the three pair of pants neatly folded, and said, "Hold your arms out." He did, and I laid three pair of size 54 pants in his arms. He was flabbergasted, and full of unbelief, but skeptical. He put the pants down, and checked the size of each pair. Then he held a pair up to himself. He was 32" in the waist. "Good Lord," he said, "I've got room in here for both of us."" "No thank you," I said. He asked, "Suppose I told you I need a new pickup truck?" I said, "Don't you dare." I saw him a few days later, and asked him if the pants fit his cook. "Yes," he said, "It was old Joe the black man, and he was so happy the Lord still loved him, and answered his prayers for two pair of pants with a bonus. So, don't think you had anything to do with those pants. The Lord provided them." Life is full of surprises and funny things if we are not too blind to see them.

I hate to leave my readers hanging, but I don't know either, what the original officer did for pants until the new contract was written. In fact, I have not heard from him again to this date.

Sometime, while writing this book, I became undecided as to whether or not I should reveal some of the things that I write about. Then I realized that most of the time, the person in question has died, so here we go.

One Saturday morning, the accountant from ACI knocked on my door in Chattahoochee, and when I went to the door, he handed me a brown paper bag with five dressed Chuker Quail in it. He lived at the bachelor quarters directly in front of the poultry project. The poultry department had been raising Chuker Quail. I had no idea what that was all about. Someone must have given the poultry supervisor some eggs. They had raised about 20 of them, but tired of the project, so they turned them loose, hoping that they would go wild and populate the area. But, no such luck. There was about a dozen hanging around the poultry houses eating the chicken feed that spilled. When the weather got cold, they could not stand it. The chicken houses had a ventilating system running along the ridge of the roof. It was letting heat escape from the chicken houses. Chicken droppings go through a heat, and it is quite warm inside of a house that has not been cleaned lately. So, the Chukers had gathered in a group at the vent on top of the chicken house right behind the bachelor quarters. Well, the temptation was too great. Those Chukers were as large as a bantam chicken. One twelve-gauge #8 shot shell, BOOM!! It rained Chukers until the count reached five. Early in the morning, no one heard the boom, or at least they ignored it. I kept the evidence in my freezer until the accountant and his pals came to get them for a barbecue. That was 30 years ago, at least, maybe 40. It was while he was still single. I know his wife would never have been living in bachelor quarters.

When my office was still at the top of the stairs, just inside the entrance of the administration building, I had more traffic than I needed or wanted. Everybody came into my office whether they had business, or just monkey business. I do not remember the reason that I had a size 54 inmate underwear shorts on my desk. They were not supposed to be there, but all sorts of things appeared on my desk. The superintendent's secretary had been a friend for more years than I care to say. In fact, she was my back door neighbor at home. She often came by my office on her way back from the control room area. This day, she came in to say hello, and spied the inmate's shorts on my desk. They looked big as a bed sheet. She picked them up, opened them, laughing all the time. Then she did the unpardonable sin. She put them on over her clothes. Then she pulled the slack out, looked down, and said, "I got room in here for you, but you can't get in here with me." All I could think of was, what would I say if the superintendent, or the director came in at that moment. I have thought of many things to say, such as "She is in the change of life", or "She is a patient from across the river," or maybe I would have said, "I don't know that person," but, since none of the above showed up, I just said nothing and enjoyed the spirit of the moment.

You will note I'm jumping from one subject to the other. That is because that is the way of life in the chain gang. Speaking of a patient from across the river, for many years, my wife and I only had one car. Sometimes we would swap rides with a clerk in my office, and his wife worked at the Florida State Hospital. My wife was a secretary for Division of Purchasing when their office was on the Florida State Hospital grounds. But then, our rides left town, so since I had to be at work before my wife, she would drop me off at the prison, then go to the mental hospital. Her family and mine too, lived back in Kentucky, and she told them about dropping me at prison and going on to the mental hospital. My dad, who was a real mountain coal miner, just looked dead faced and said, "God bless you, my children."

Some of the most pleasant experiences I had during my stint in the chain gang was the relationships that I established with the vendors. It's hard to keep friendships with vendors in proper prospective. They always want to do more personal things for you that may not be proper. I had some vendors that ate lunch with me once a month. The problem I had with that, was that they wanted to pay for the meal every time. One salesman was with Bernard Foods, the other with Peddie Chemicals. They were friends before they started selling to me. The Peddie salesman came to my office at lunch. The Bernard man had come to my office early, then went on to call on other clients, and met the two of us at a little cafe in Sneads. For years, we did that, and I told them I would pay for the meal every third month, or I would not meet with them.

I finally got them to agree to it, but they never were happy with the deal.

The Peddie Chemical man just lived close by between here and Tallahassee. We hunted together and went to FSU ball games. I did wood carvings for him. In fact, I made a 12 inch statue of him. After we both retired, in fact he came to my retirement party, he became very ill. On his birthday, I went to visit him in the hospital and carried a bream buster fishing pole as a birthday gift. The next day he passed away. His wife called and told me that my friend died and that he had requested that I preach his funeral. I had never done that before, but I did it for him.

There were other vendors that I met and cared a lot for. I remember back in 1972, there was a gas and oil shortage. The Department of General Services, Division of Purchasing made annual contracts with major oil companies to deliver gasoline to the prisons. They told us there was nothing that they could do. When we run out of gas, we would just have to walk. Well, I called my good friend at Standard Oil in Marianna, and asked him what could be done. He said, "Don't you fret, I'm not going to let you run short of gas." He said he would fill out some forms that the government required him to fill out, and users had to sign. He said, "I'll send them to you by my delivery driver. Just sign them and I'll do the rest." Well, he was as good as his word.

Almost a year later, we were in a meeting with the purchasing people, and they asked me what I had done to get by during the gasoline crunch. In front of the whole purchasing staff of the prisons in Florida, I asked, "What did you do for me?" "Nothing," they said. "Well, I'm going to do the same. I'm going to tell you nothing except that I never ran out of gas, and I didn't ever have to stand in line at the pump," I said.

My boss in Tallahassee said, "Boy, you had a lot of nerve to tell those guys that." "I always tell the truth, or at least almost all the time," I said.

It was in one of the annual meetings one day when we were about ready to leave for lunch. One of the older purchasing agents said, "I've been here for 13 years. I wonder if anyone has been here longer." The person holding the class looked around and said, "How about you, P.A. at Raiford State Prison?" He answered, "17 years". I was sitting in the rear of the class next to the purchasing director from central office in Tallahassee. He looked at me and grinned. Then the instructor asked, "Anyone been here longer?" Then he spotted me and asked, "How about you Cliff?" I meekly said, "28". The teacher said, "Aw, hell, let's go to lunch."

I was the oldest purchasing agent in seniority for 16 years when I finally retired with 38 years' service.

I didn't like to go to those state purchasing agent meetings. They took a week out of my office time, and it was all I could do to keep up without that interruption. I told my boss, the director of purchasing for the Department of Corrections, "They didn't know enough to tell me anything." He said, "I don't doubt that. So why don't you come on and share some of that knowledge with the new guys on the block?" I said, "I would be glad to. Just give me a spot on the program." He asked, "Do you think I'm crazy? You would have everyone on my neck from the Governor on down." He was my best buddy in all those people in Tallahassee, and he knew it too. He didn't mind calling on me when he needed me.

My daughter is a dental hygienist and cleaned his teeth. She introduced him to the other dental staff, as my boss. His reply was, "Oh, nobody is HIS boss."

I saw him at the funeral service for my good friend, the business manager at ACI. This man was also the good friend of the director, who is also now retired.

This director was the best leader of men that I ever knew. His theory was, "give him enough rope, and he will hang himself if he is wrong. If he is right, he will tangle his feet up, and realize he is pushing too hard."

I will never forget his 40th birthday. He was over visiting the regional office in Marianna. The day before, he called the administrative assistant, and told him he was coming. The ad. assist. called me and asked me to get a cake and a present, and he would bring the director over to my office at ACI. I had my wife to bake him a cake and decorate it. It said, "Happy 60th Birthday", but it was really his 40th. I got him a nice ball point pen, but the main big present was a commode seat and cover cut in half right down the center and spray painted gold. I put a tag on it that said, "For my half-assed rich friend." He kept it in his office he said.

When I retired, he came to my party, and gave me a garnet and gold T-shirt that said, "Ex-owner and operator of ACI," and my main gift from him was that same half of a commode seat painted gold. He put a new tag on it that said the same thing it said when I gave it to him.

There must have been some pranks or jokes that I pulled on someone or someone pulled on me. But I forgot some of them.

Some of the fun times were when the staff at ACI got together and went dove hunting. I remember one day we all gathered up at one of the employees' houses in Sneads. It was a little early, and we were sitting down on the front lawn. I looked over at the superintendent who had on a pair of tennis shoes. He was laying down on his side with one foot laying on top of the other. I said, "Good Lord! What size are those shoes?" He said, "13. These shoes caused me to get my butt whipped by my wife. They gave me these when I was going to college at the University of Florida. They told me if I got them wet, to keep them on until they dried, or they would shrink up so that I couldn't get them on again. Well, when it got time to go to bed that night I got wet, the shoes were not dry, so I got into bed with the wet tennis shoes on. That is when she kicked my butt." I believe that was a true story knowing him.

I've been sitting here thinking over the years, and I thought of certain groups of people. The group I now have on my mind were three of the psychologists that were with us during my time. The first one was a typical psychologist. He was being used as a counselor. One inmate that was very depressed was sent to him for counseling, afterwards on his way to the dormitory, he slit his wrist with a razor blade at 3:00 pm The second psychologist cut the legs off of his bed in the bachelor quarters because he could not breathe. It was 8 inches high.

The third psychologist had an office chair that he could not lean back in because the springs were broken, and he would flip over. He wrote a note to the superintendent and said that sitting in the chair was like trying to ride a bucking bronco. The superintendent passed the letter on to me to see if I could solve his problem. When I got the letter, I responded to his letter and told him that we had some saddles at the farm he could borrow to ride that bucking chair. We also had at the maintenance shop, some half-inch rope that his secretary could use to tie him into the chair. Also, we had a source in the canteen where he could order a set of spurs to keep that chair under control. I said, if none of these were satisfactory, he could submit a purchase request, and I could buy him a new chair. Finally, I said for him to please let me know what option he chose. He selected the option to submit a request for a new chair. I flagged the assistant superintendent with a copy of the letter, and that assist. superintendent left and was promoted to Supt. at another institution. I saw him 10 years later at one of the purchasing agents' conferences and the first thing he said to me was that he still had a copy of that letter I wrote to the psychologist about the bucking chair. He said he laughed every time he thought about it.

Sometime in the 1980s the Tallahassee office decided they would lighten my work load and hire a regional purchasing director to purchase for all the road camps, probation centers, regional office, work camps, and the like. They advertised the job for all the state. Everyone in the world just knew that I would be the one to get the job because it would be a promotion and pay raise for me. When a big decision arises in my life, I always get a pencil or pen and a sheet of paper, and list two columns, one pro and one con. I list all advantages in one column and disadvantages in the other. When I did that for this job, listed were promotion and pay raise in the advantages. I had a dozen or more listed under disadvantages, such as driving 50 miles every day, cost of gas and oil, and repairs to my car, extra hour at least each day to and from work, and it went on and on. So, I just threw the application in the trash can. At 4 pm on the day that the advertising would close, the administrative assistant from the regional office called me and said, "Cliff, I haven't received your application for the regional purchasing director's job yet." I said, "Oh, my gosh, and it's 4:00 pm! How can I get it over there in that little time? Oh my. What can I do? This is terrible." And I went on and on, until he said, "Aw, knock it off! You didn't even apply. Why don't you take it?" I told him I had evaluated it, and I would loose money and time. I had my retirement almost made so I decided to let it pass. Then he threw me a curve I could not believe. He said, "How about your coming over here and helping me and the head accountant choose a placement for the position?" I asked, "Do you realize you are asking me to choose my boss?" He said, "That doesn't make any difference. There is no one in the region that knows anything about purchasing. We have relied fully on you, and I would like you to question the applicants to determine whether or not they are qualified, and also, I want you to cooperate and help whoever we choose." I tried to think of a situation where a person was asked to sit in on the committee to hire their boss, and I never heard of such a thing. Well, I did what he requested. There were three applicants, and only one was even close to being qualified. I voted for her, and the other two went along. The strangest thing happened. That "hussy" turned on me with a vengeance that only a she-devil could have. I never could determine her motive. When I asked her what was her point, she only said, "Doing my job." I said, "Let me tell you something, I was here when you came and I'll be here when you leave." And I was. I never did hear all of what happened, but she was transferred to another region within two years. I know that the central office in Tallahassee where I had numerous friends knew of the situation in Region one between her and me. I heard in a couple of years, that she had died. I felt sorry about the loss, but I wasn't interested enough to ask any questions. My Grandpa, a hillbilly from Kentucky used to say, "Let the sleeping dog lay."

Now I can tell it. I was offered bribes many times to break the laws. One time a chemical company heard from somewhere that I was looking for 13 colored television sets for the inmate dormitories. They were to be bought from the Inmate Welfare Fund. An account that the State Purchasing Commission will not spend because it is not state funds. The money is accumulated by selling goods to inmates for more than we pay for them with 20% profit. The inmates' relatives send them money. It is put in their bank accounts. They can only spend it in the canteen unless they get special permission from the committee on canteen activities. You might say we have a captive audience. A great deal of money had accumulated by this time, so the funds were available. The inmates had black and white televisions already, but some "bleeding hearts" came up with the idea to change them out for color sets. I was told verbally to get them. I forgot, since I did not have it in writing. I was a "dyed in the wool redneck disciplinarian." I said, "None of our guys got in here for singing too loud in Sunday School." In my opinion, they had it too good, and besides, I only had a black and white TV at home, and I couldn't afford a colored TV then. I could drag my feet because I didn't have it in writing. eighteen months later, the big mouthed education director was over in Tallahassee brown nosing, and heard the director talking about the inmates enjoying color TV's, and our education director said, "Well, our inmates don't have color TV because our purchasing agent only has a black and white set." "Well," said the director, "I'll take care of that today." He wrote me a letter directing me to purchase the color TV sets.

I've chased enough rabbits to get around to why I was buying color TV sets. This chemical company had a furniture store as well as a chemical warehouse. The salesman said to me, "Purchase the 13 sets from me, and I'll set one in your living room free." I said, as I laid back in my chair looking at the clock, "You have five minutes to get to the parking lot, and be gone. If not, I'm calling the security chief, and have you arrested for attempted bribery." It only took 1-1/2 minutes for him to be scratching off. Evidently he must have heard me yell as he ran down the stairs, "And don't let me see you back here again!"

There was another time for attempted bribery. There was an office supplies salesman who kept calling me from California wanting to sell office supplies. Every time he called, he was looking for sympathy. One time he said his wife had just died. Another time, he said his daughter had been raped, and his warehouse had been flooded by the storm. His prices were so high, I would not buy from him. He had a squeaky voice that no one could mistake, so as soon as I would answer the phone, "Cliff Gilley" He would say, "Mr. Cleef?" I knew it was him, and for a long time, I would say, "Hello, hello, hello.....Aw heck, this phone is dead again" I would hear him say, "No, Mr. Cleef, I can hear you." I would hang up the phone. He would do it three times before he would give up. Much later, I was in a sympathetic mood, and I let him talk. Surprisingly enough, when I asked his price on electric typewriter ribbons, his price was two cents each, cheaper than our local dealer. So, I ordered two dozen ribbons. We had several typewriters that used those ribbons. Well, I gave him a purchase order, and soon the ribbons arrived, just like a sensible vendor would do, but when the invoice came into the business office, they called me and asked, "Mr. Gilley, do you want me to pay this shipping and handling charge for $150 on the typewriter ribbons? Your purchase order says F.O.B. Destination." I said, "I'll be right up there." I went to the clerk's office and she handed me the invoice. I just put it down on the desk, and marked, "F.O.B. Destination, and marked out the shipping and handling charge, signed my name on it, and said, "Now pay it." I couldn't believe what I had just seen. That day, when I got home, I had a small letter just addressed to Cliff Gilley, Chattahoochee Florida with no return address on it. My wife asked, "How did it get here?" I said, "I know all those guys in the post office. They just sent it right out." Then, when I opened it, guess what? A check from my vendor in California for $75.00 was inside, made out to "cash". I realized then, that was half of the shipping and handling charge. I didn't wait for anything the next morning. I wrote him a letter and said, "I'm returning your bribing check for $75, and if you ever call me again, I'm going to turn this file over to the FBI in Tallahassee." I made a copy of the check and the letter for my personnel file. One for the business office manager, and one for the superintendent, and I have never heard from anyone on this subject since then. I must have handled it OK.

I did not use any diagram or plan or foundation for writing this book. I just jump from one subject to the other. I just remembered something that happened on a trip to Orlando to a purchasing and food service conference. The food service in the central office in Tallahassee decided to include themselves in purchasing conferences, which was fine with me. They had their own classes and meetings separate from ours, but we all met and stayed in the same hotel. This year, we had five from this area to go in our vehicle. Four of us doubled up in rooms, and cut the cost in half. The food service director at East unit, and I were good friends, so we stayed together. The purchasing agent from River Junction Correctional Institution and his food service director roomed together. That left the food service director at West Unit at ACI to stay by himself. We were staying at the Radison Hotel. The two ACI cooks and I planned to go out to eat about 7:30 pm. We were down in the lobby, sitting and visiting until time to go out and eat. We decided to go back up to our room and freshen up before going out for dinner. When we met back down in the lobby, the West unit food service director said, "Somebody has been in my room. They messed the bed up, and left a Hershey candy bar on my pillow." I must tell you about our West unit friend. I don't think he had ever been out of Jackson County before, much less, stayed in a fancy hotel. I asked him what he did with the candy. He said, "I ate it." "Oh, no," I asked, "You know what that means?" "No." he said.

I said, "Well, that was left there by a call girl, and the fact that you ate the candy, means that you want a call girl to come back at midnight." He said, "What kind?" I said, "Well, some black, some Mexican, few white." He said, "I don't mind a white, but none other." I asked, "What did you do with the paper from the candy?" He said, "I left it laying on the desk." "Oh, my!" I said. He asked, "Why? What does that mean?" I said, "That means that you are willing to pay cash." He said, "I didn't bring that kind of cash money with me." I said, "They don't take credit cards." "Then, she is out of luck," he said. "No" I said, "You are out of luck." He said, "If she comes, I won't let her in." "She has a pass key, and will come on in," I said. "I'll throw her out," he said. My turn again, "Don't try that, because her body guard, and pimp will be right behind her, a big ugly dude." We went on out to dinner and had a very pleasant time. When we got back to our room, the West Unit cook came in too. We sat and talked for about an hour, and I got ready for bed. I went to bed, and soon was asleep. About 4:00 in the am, I needed to go to the bathroom, and some light was coming from a street light into our room. I almost choked when I saw the West Unit cook lying on a coffee table with his feet in a chair. He had taken the East Unit cook's bed spread and covered the table and chair, and slept the whole night in our room. When I woke up in the morning, he was gone. When my roommate woke up, I asked, "What happened to West Unit?" He replied, "He said he was not going to stay up there, and asked me if he could sleep in the bed with me." I said, "No way, you got a bed upstairs, and I don't suggest you get in the bed with Cliff, although he deserves it." Well, West Unit never did act any different toward me, nor mention anything about that incident, except he told East Unit, that he did not eat any more of that candy.

CHAPTER 7
SLOWING DOWN

As I look back over the many years, I find myself remembering the good things, and good times instead of the bad ones. I really loved to attend the annual picnic and barbecue supplied by the state. Although I purchased for both units, East and West, I would go for a year sometimes without seeing some of the West unit people. The annual picnic was an excuse to get together and keep relationships warm. It was a splendid time for keeping normal relationships between the East and West unit staff. These picnics were held away from the Institution, at a state park. Later, a staff training building was built, and also used for the annual picnics. There was another event that was held on the state lands that I enjoyed, although only about 12 to 15 men were all that participated in it. That was an organized and planned dove shoot. Sometimes three or four a year. They were always held on a work day. The inmates were kept away from the field where the shoots were being held. The most popular and successful were held in the millet field directly in front of the administration building. You could only shoot doves in the afternoons. Many times I would bring my hunting clothes and gun, and shells in the trunk of my car. I would go get my hunting clothes out of the trunk of my car, and put them on over my work clothes. White shirt and tie were my work clothes. I would take my bag lunch with me, and go out into the field to my favorite spot under the power line. I would sit on my five gallon bucket that has a rotating seat for a lid. I would be ready to start shooting at 1 pm. Many times, the doves would start flying early, and they loved to fly by the power line coming in the field to feed. Several times, I would kill my 12 bird limit, pick the feathers off of them, put them into my paper bag which had held my lunch, and then go back to the office. I would put the birds in my office refrigerator. It took about an hour and a half, and I would finish out the day working. I would take my hunting clothes off, and leave them in my car in the parking lot in front of the building. One year we received complaints that the bird shots that we were firing into the air toward the ball field where the inmates who were on "off duty" were playing. The pellets were falling on the field, and scared them because they thought the pellets would hurt them. So we just moved the shooting zone a little further into the field away from the compound, and marked the edge of the hunting zone with yellow flags. I always enjoyed being included in the hunts.

There was an organized hunt one time at a corn field close to the dairy on the lake. The birds were coming across the lake where they had rested during noon time. The lake front had huge trees along it. The birds would swoop down into the field as soon as they cleared the trees. It was agreed that everyone would refrain from shooting low flying birds to keep from shooting someone. Well, on this day, a young inexperienced guy was following a bird with his gun, and as soon as it swooped down low over the field, he fired. I was about 50 yards away looking toward him, and could see him aim and swoop with the bird. As soon as I heard the shot, I felt the five pellets hit me. The most painful one was the one that hit my hand where I was holding the gun forearm, and pinched the skin against my gun. I yelled at him, "You have shot me, you stupid jerk!" One pellet hit me on the right cheek bone, and penetrated the skin, one on the chin bone which also penetrated the skin, two hit me on the neck breaking the skin, but did not penetrate my skin. I put my hand to my face and when I pulled it away, it was bloody. I immediately gathered my paraphernalia up, and started back to the institution. We had a medical infirmary, and I knew there would be a medical technician on duty, so that is where I headed. As I went through the administration building to get to the infirmary, I must have met a dozen people. Everyone saw a bloody face, and everyone asked, "What happened?" I said, "I got shot, but you should see the other guy." Sure enough, there was an intern medical tech. on duty. He was scared to death when I walked in until I told him it wouldn't require surgery. Just two shots penetrated the skin. Get your tweezers and pluck them out. First he got some alcohol on a swab and cleaned the blood away. I told him I wanted to save the shots for a keepsake. He picked the shot out of my right cheek first. And, as he was showing me that he had it, he dropped it down inside my shirt collar and we never found the thing. But, on the one in my chin, we saved it. I glued it on my key chain and saved it for years. Finally, it fell off. The guy that shot me came to the car as I was leaving the dove field and asked me what happened. I said, "You hit me, you fool." He denied shooting me. I guess he was afraid I would sue him or something worse. He has never admitted the shot, but I knew it was an accident. I just thank God it was far enough away to be no worse than it was. The medical technician that performed the delicate surgery left state employment for postal service in Chattahoochee, and is now Postmaster. A couple of years ago, I saw him and his wife in the Dr.'s office in Tallahassee, and asked him if he remembered picking shots out of my face. He agreed that he did remember, and told me he had another after that which was not nearly as successful since it was in the other end, and the patient yelled a lot more!!!

Going back a little way, I forgot to tell you something that was a bit entertaining to me. While our office was still in the warehouse, we had a shipment of musical instruments received from a vendor in Tallahassee. When he delivered them, I was in the warehouse and signed a delivery receipt for the delivery. He asked me if we would like to have a couple of guitars that were broken beyond repair, for free. He said he was going to throw them away. I said, "Yes." He gave them to me. They were beautiful, perfectly new, shiny and bright. I asked what was wrong with them. He showed me that both had loose, and broken necks. He said if you tried to tune them, you would just break the neck off. I said, "I'll have some fun out of these." I knew that the chief cook used to play the guitar. He always walked down the hallway from the kitchen to the warehouse to see what was going on every morning. I was loaded for him. I had one of the guitars on my desk. When he walked in, he spied that pretty thing laying on my desk. He asked, "Mr. Gilley, where did you get this thing?" I asked, "You want to touch it?" He started to pick it up. I said, "No, don't pick it up, just touch it." He asked, "Why can't I pick it up?" I said, "Because it's not yours yet. Would you like to buy it?" "No," he said, "I have all the music makers I want." Then my salesmanship clicked in, "Don't you think it's pretty?" "Yep," he replied. "You say you have all the guitars you need? Well, what would you give to own this pretty thing?" "Not much," he said. "How much is not much, $50?" "Oh, no," he said, "much less than that." "$25?" I asked. "Oh, no" he said, "Much less than that." "Like what?" I asked. "No more than five "bucks" he said. "Sold," I said, "How would you like to pay?" "Cash," he said. He gave me a five dollar bill, and took the guitar with a look that said, "Got you that time stupid." When he left, I said, "He'll be back.'"

One down and one to go I thought. I took the other guitar out to the warehouse and put it on a table out there that was used to wrap packages. I stood by to see who would be my next victim. Well, I didn't have to wait long. The good friend who ran the print shop came in and asked me what was happening? I said, "We are running a special today for five dollars you can have this beautiful musical instrument." I was just having some fun. I knew the man would not fall for this trick. Even if he did, I would not let it happen. But, what I didn't know was, listening in the tool department was a person that everyone called "Mr. know it all" He was listening to me try and sell my good buddy a beautiful guitar. "Mr. know it all" walked up beside me and said, "I bid $15". He threw a five and a ten dollar bill down on the table, took the guitar, and out the door he went. I raised my eyebrows, looked at my friend, and burst out laughing. He asked, "What are you up to?" I said, "That thing has a broken neck, and can't be played."

Later I saw that guitar in a store window down at River Junction with a $25 price tag on it. It stayed there for years, and I don't believe it was ever sold.

Now, back to the first guitar that the chief cook purchased. Just as I predicted, that afternoon, "Mr. food service" came back to my office and said, "I tried to tune that guitar, and it won't tune because it has a broken neck." I said, "You remember telling a group of us the other day that no one could slick you? When you were watering your yard, and an encyclopedia salesman kept on bothering you after telling him three times you were not interested, you turned your hose on him." I handed him back his five dollars and said, "Sir, you have just been slicked, and for being such a good sport, your prize is that you may keep that old broken-necked guitar." By reading this book, it must seem to you that I was always the prankster doing others in, well, I have a real gift of being able to forget the times that I was on the receiving end of pranks.

I have stood and watched hundreds of inmates walk by and said to myself, and sometimes to others, "What a waste of man power."

There have been some talented men who pulled time in our institution. I must share this with you. A group of spiritual and religious people decided that the West Unit needed a place to worship. The East Unit had church services in the school auditorium. It worked out really well. But, the inmates only had a small office building to worship in at the West Unit, so the West Unit chaplain and some outside church groups began a program to furnish funds to have a church chapel built inside the compound at the West Unit. For several years, various people, businesses, manufacturers and churches were contacted, and the chaplain at the West Unit made contact with state officials to secure permission, and clear the way for this building to be built with inmate labor, and officers to instruct the inmates as part of the assignment.

The bank president of the Sneads branch bank was contacted, and asked to write checks against the building account in his bank that held all the contributions. In turn, the chaplain asked me to purchase the materials by purchase order, and to authorize payment of all invoices. I got permission from my superintendent, and away we went to build a chapel for the West Unit. I told you all of that to tell you about the ability of the inmates. that worked so hard to complete this building. I had an electrical salesman who called on me each Tuesday, and I asked him several times to go by the chapel and help them decide what exactly they needed for the job. One day he went by the chapel, before coming to my office. He said, "They had the 200 amp box installed, and had not covered it up yet, and he examined this work, and asked the officer in charge who did this work? It's beautiful." The officer pointed to an inmate. The salesman asked the inmate, "What are you doing in here?" The inmate replied, "I'm not in here for not being able to do my job."

One inmate requested that he be permitted to blow glitter on the ceiling as they were painting, while the paint was still wet. He wanted to use a leaf blower and make a funnel out of poster board and blow glitter onto the wet paint. They gave him permission to do this. I went to the dedication ceremony for the building, and it gave you the feeling that you were out in the starlit night.

Every time I see that chapel building now, I think of the chaplain who has passed away, and how diligent he was in building that building. When the building was completed, it had to be given to the state, because it was on state property. It was built by state inmates, and so, it would be covered by state insurance. It may belong to the state now, but the inmates know to whom it belongs. They said they gave it to God.

CHAPTER 8
<u>INDUSTRIES' PROBLEMS</u>

An audit showed that the poultry project lost $40,000 one year, and was in need of some changes. The industries' manager came to me for help. I wondered why he didn't go to the business manager, and then I knew why. I told him I would try. We had been purchasing feed supplement from a chemical company in Chicago, so I called him. He had been in our office several times on public relations trips. He was delighted that I called him. He was a chemical analyst specialist. I made the remark a lot of times that he was the smartest man I had ever met. He said, "I've been looking for an excuse to come to Florida, so I'll see you next week." He was one of seven men that the federal government used as scientists. He and I sat down at my desk. I asked the industries' manager if he wanted to come in and see a genius, and a blockhead at work. He said, "Just give me a report on what you want me to do."

The first question the scientist asked me was what kind of a lighting program we had our hens on. I said, "24 hours a day." "Oh, gosh." he said. "Get you a $12 timer, and give the hens 6-8 hours of sleep a night. When they are asleep, they are not eating and wasting food." He asked me what method of measuring the

$38 per pound of vitamin supplement they were selling us. I said, "A coffee can full." He said, "Any more than a pound per ton is wasted. Who puts it in the mixer," he asked? I said, "An inmate". "costly," he said. He also suggested that we get a premix to put in our feed, rather than take a chance on mixing the feed with all those expensive chemicals. Just mix 6 bags of premix per ton, and your cost will drop a noticeable amount. We discussed several more changes that should be made. I told him I had a question. "How long does a hen live?" He said, "Why do you ask that?" I said, "My daughter has a pet hen that is 6 years old, and I wonder how much longer she can expect to have the chicken." Well," he said, "That is why I like to come see you, because I learn so much. I have never heard of a hen living that long. All the hens I deal with, when they quit laying, they go to Campbell's Chicken Soup. Please let me know how long she lives." The hen lived to be seven and a half years old. I called the scientist when she died.

To make a long story short, I helped the industries' manager get all the changes made, and in six months, the poultry department made $40,000 per month instead of losing it.

The industries' manager was so tickled with the results that he bought me and my secretary lunch one day.

We got into an interesting work some years ago. When the state changed from getting metal vehicle license plates every year, to getting a new one every five years, someone had to print the 13 million decals to put on the old plates for the four years in-between. Well, they said in Tallahassee, Apalachee has only 19 industries, give them another one. Give them a validation sticker plant, and they did. At the time we opened our validation sticker print plant, there were 13 million licensed vehicles in the State of Florida. So, our first year, we were to make that many stickers. Never in my life, had I dealt with those kinds of figures. So, when I ordered the rolls of envelopes to put them in, I ordered all 13 million at one time. Not thinking how much space a roll of envelopes can take up, when the shipment came in, my warehouse foreman called me and said, "What do you want me to do with all these plastic envelopes you ordered?" I said, "Just put them there in the warehouse, and call the sticker plant and have them pick them up". He replied, "you better come over here and see what you have bought." I did, and when I saw a semi-truck load of pallets loaded with a half a million on each pallet, and counted the 26 pallets, I said, "Golly Molly." I had no idea what I was ordering. I looked around, saw a wide aisle, and said, "Line them up in this aisle, and I'll encourage the sticker plant to use them up and get them out as fast as they can." It was a little inconvenient, but no big deal. We got a big laugh about that as long as I worked.

I was amazed when we figured out how much money was involved in making validation stickers. It cost us two and a half cents to make each sticker, which amounted to $325,000. We sold them to the 65 Florida counties for five cents each, which amounted to $650,000. Quite a profitable business, and lovely amount of money to put into the industrial trust fund. But, getting those things delivered to 65 different locations was a problem. It was 500 miles to the farthest county office. The counties paid 5 cents each for the stickers, and sold them for an average of $32 per sticker. We used two officers to deliver the stickers, one to drive and one to ride shotgun. Because the face value of the stickers ran up into billions of dollars. None of the local deliveries like UPS, or FedEx could handle them. When one of the drivers got to a county office before it opened, rather than wait for them to come open up, he just left two cases of 90,000 stickers on the sidewalk and drove off. When the county workers came to work and found that stuff sitting on the sidewalk, they pitched a fit, called our institution, and needless to say, that driver did not drive for us any more.

CHAPTER 9
MISCELLANEOUS FINALS

The last three years that I worked, I used a computer, and although I had a secretary, she also used a computer. But, there were way too many purchase orders for her to put into the system. She and I both went to Panama City, Florida to learn how to use the computer. They gave us each a book that we could use and keep. All the expense of sending us down there was not necessary because, until we learned the method which took about three weeks, we went step by step using the book.

One day, I had run several purchase orders into the system, and printed them out. My secretary came into my office carrying a purchase order that she had taken out of the printer which was in her office, and she said, "I think you may have made a mistake. Are you sure you want to purchase $500,000 worth of toilet paper?" I looked at it and realized that my computer did not automatically put in the decimal point. I really wanted $5,000 worth, not half a million. But, I wouldn't let her have the pleasure of catching me in an error, so I said, "Don't sweat it. I'll just order a semi-truck load of Caster Oil, and we'll use up that paper in a couple of weeks." She said, "I'll correct it for you."

I saw last night an educational show on the History Channel about the Atica Prison riot, and said, "Thank goodness our institution wasn't like that." You remember I told you before that we were minimum security? We only had first offenders and they were between ages 14 and 24. They were mean little boogers, but not hardened criminals like those at Atica. We did have our riots. I was right in the middle of one in the 1970's. We had just been integrated. I came in to work and saw little groups of people talking in excited, hushed voices. I went over to one group and asked, "What's going on?" The speaker said, "We had one killed last night in the dorm." I wanted the details, and this was what I heard. A little 150 pound white boy went to a lieutenant last week and said, "You had better move that big black guy to another dorm. He tried to rape me in the shower last night. If he tries it again, and lays a hand on me, I'll kill him." Well, I never knew who the lieutenant was, and didn't want to know, but he did nothing about it. Last night, the black guy who weighed over 200 pounds, grabbed the white guy to rape him from behind. The white guy had a six inch blade hunting knife that his mother had slipped into him on visiting day last Sunday. He just turned the point of the knife upward, put the knife behind him with the tip pointed backward a bit, and struck an upward blow. The point of the knife entered the attacker's stomach just below the rib cage, and hit the heart at the bottom. He bled to death before they could get him out of the dorm. They took the kid that did the killing and locked him up in confinement for protective custody. Three days later, a bunch of blacks were gathered on a dorm porch, and a white inmate came up on the porch. One said, "They killed one of our brothers. Let's kill one of them." They ganged up on the white guy and beat him almost to death before the officers could break it up. At noon that day, a few hours later, a bunch of white men said, "Let's thin the blacks out." After they finished lunch, they went down to the engineering department and armed themselves with hammers, axes, and any deadly thing they could find. They came up into the area in front of the dining hall. The blacks had gotten word, and went into the construction warehouse, and armed themselves. there were blacks on one side of the ten foot wide sidewalks, and whites on the other side, shouting at each other. I was in the administration building shooting pool after I ate my bag lunch. A guard came into the recreational room and yelled, "Out back, you guys, they need you. There's a riot." There were just two of us there. Usually there are 12-15 men in there. We ran up the steps to the control office. The guard asked, "Do you want a gun?" I said, "No, I don't want to kill anyone. Just give me a night stick." They gave me a good heavy one. The other man with me got a night stick also. When we opened the door at the back of the building, I said, "Oh, Lord, let's go." I ran hard as I could which was pretty fast. As soon as I got between the first black and white inmates, I shouted, "On the ground, all of you!" I first pointed my stick at the blacks, and they didn't move. I drew the stick over my head, and said, "I said, sit down!" A few sat down, and then I turned to the whites, and went through the same motions. A few whites sat down. Then, as I walked up the sidewalks, between the blacks and whites, I kept yelling, "On the ground!" All of them looked at me like I was crazy. A few had something to say about why they were there. I said, "Knock it off! That means everyone just shut up." With all my yelling, and swinging that night stick, they all quieted down and sat down. I then said to myself, "What do I do now?" I saw a guard on the sidewalk and yelled at him to get us some help out here. I didn't know how long I could hold them, but it didn't take long before we had guards swarming everywhere. After it was all over and the security had the men locked up, I thought, that was a crazy thing to do. But, that is part of my job. Although I was a purchasing agent, my first responsibility was to keep the inmates secured, and second to keep the peace, and protect the state's property. I think the reason I was successful, was that the blacks were outnumbered, and didn't want to get the heck beat out of them, and the whites felt I was on their side because I was white. Also, we had only the best inmates in the State of Florida, because the best inmates were sent to us.

They were young and had not had time to get hardened, and they were all first offenders.

I had seen the captain of the guard do his thing one day after lunch, with a group of about 50 men. They decided they were not going to work that afternoon. When they were told to fall out for work call, they shouted, "We will not work."

It was just about 50 yards from the captain's office to the dining hall. The chief cook called him and told him of the situation. He said, "I'll be right there." In just a matter of minutes he walked in through the back door, and everybody became real quiet. As he walked up to the front of the dining hall, he made quite an impression. He weighed about 230 pounds, but wasn't very tall. He had a head and neck like a bulldog. He looked around and decided who was in charge of the sit down, and climbed up on top of the stainless steel table, looked around and asked, "What's the trouble, fellas?" The ring leader said, "We are not going to work today. It's too hot." The captain said, "You are either going to work or get buried." He pulled that 45-caliber revolver that he had strapped on his side, pointed it right between the leader's eyes, cocked the hammer back, and said, "When I say go, if you don't go, I'm going to pull this trigger. Now go!" The whole crew acted like a covey of quail. Within one minute, all that was left was the staff. I said, "If the captain could do that, so could I."

I was not present when the attempt at escaping was made. Our poultry supervisor was the strongest man I knew. He was 6'5" tall, weighed about 200 pounds, and hard as blue twisted steel. He drove a covered pickup truck hauling inmates to and from poultry about a quarter of a mile away from checkout point. One day he was driving his truck loaded with inmates in the back and one inmate in the cab with him. When he started to turn in at the East Gate, the inmate put a knife in his side, and told him to keep on driving straight ahead. Well, the officer with hands as big as 20-pound hams reached over and caught the inmate by the wrist, and with a grip like a vise, forced his hand down toward the floor board, and forced the man to drop the knife. He turned in at the East Gate, stopped the truck, snatched the inmate out on the pavement, and said to the control officer, "You need this man. He just tried to capture me with this knife." When I heard this, I said, "Of all the men employed at ACI, that is the worst choice he could have made. They should give him three additional years for extreme stupidity."

One day I was sitting at my desk at the top of the stairs in the administration building when the superintendent came from his office to my open door and said, "Come go with me." I didn't say anything. I just got up and followed him to the parking lot. Out front, we got in his personal state car, and sped off toward highway 90. I didn't ask any questions, knowing he would tell me where we were going when the time came. When we got to Highway 90, he turned left, then he said, "We have an inmate stuck in the soap machine." I said, "Oh no. That is serious business. That machine is a1,000 pound capacity with three blades turning over and over, turned by a 50 horsepower motor." When we got there and walked over to the soap mixer, it was anchored below the floor of the soap factory down 8 steps to the work floor. The top of the mixer was a little over knee high where the top of the machine had a large door. The chemicals were loaded in the top and mixed, and when mixed, were bagged or canned from the small door at the bottom. When we went over to the machine and looked into it, it was so dark, I could not make out for a long time what was in there. Then I realized there was a black man's body with no clothes on. The blades had turned him over and over until it had scrubbed his clothes off. The blades were one across his mid section, and another one had his right leg. I figured that he was dead. We had a local Dr. on payroll to take care of our inmates. The supervisor at the soap factory said the Dr. was on his way. I realized we would need him if we could get the man out. We removed the V-belt from the motor so we could turn the mixing paddles without having to turn the motor. By this time, the Dr. and a medical tech. had arrived. When the Dr. came in and looked down into the mixer, he just shook his head, but when he spoke to the trapped inmate, he answered and told the Dr. that he was not in a lot of pain, mostly just felt pressure. The Dr. was a big man well over 6', and 200 pounds, and the med. tech. was even bigger than the Dr. The opening in the top of the mixer was large enough for both of them to put the upper part of their body into the mixer. The Dr. said, "The first thing we have to do, is to get him out of there before he panics." The Dr. told the med. tech., "Come on, and help me turn the paddle wheels." They both took hold of the metal mixing paddles, which were long pieces of curved metal and pulled with all their might. The trapped man didn't say a word. With great pressure, the two huge men managed to turn the shaft, and we were able to pull the inmate out the top of the mixer. We had discussed the options as to how to get him out. We even thought of cutting him out with a torch, but abandoned that idea. We even thought about disassembling the mixer, but that would take too long. When the two medical men just peeled him out, like peeling an apple, I said, "See, there's nothing to it." We laid the freed inmate down on the concrete floor, his right leg was ground off just above the ankle, and was only hanging by some skin. His lower intestines were hanging out, but they weren't bleeding, nor did they look like they had been ruptured. The Dr. took a clean towel, and folded it, and told me to hold his intestines in until the ambulance came. He examined his broken leg, and just shook his head. Only a few minutes later, the ambulance came on, rushed him to the Tallahassee hospital. There was hardly any blood at all. I asked the Dr., "Why?" He said, "The pressure of the paddles had restricted the blood vessels. He'll bleed plenty if that ambulance driver, and med. tech don't take good care of him. Well, he lived. He lost that leg, and had to spend a long time in the hospital at Raiford. Later on, he sued the state for not having a grill covering the top of the mixing machine. But, after investigating his statement, that he had been up on the mixer cleaning it when he fell into it while it was on. But, eyewitnesses testified that he and another inmate would catch the officer in charge away from the plant, one of the men would climb into the mixer, wrap himself around the shaft, and yell OK. The other one would turn it on, and he would ride the shaft for a thrill.

They did weld a grill mesh over the opening in the top of the mixer, so the court did not award the injured inmate any reward for his stupidity. The last I heard from him, he was still in prison. I don't know where he is now. Of course, that was 23 years ago now. He may be dead.

There was an old black inmate at the farm program driving a tractor when I came to work in 1958. They said he was the best tractor driver in the state prison system. When his expiration of sentence ended, he didn't want to go away. He had no family or friends on the outside, and said that no one would hire a black ex con. So what could he do? Well, he decided what to do. He walked down the street of a large town in Florida, picked up a brick, and with a police officer looking right at him, he threw the brick through a store window. Within 30 days, he was back at ACI on his tractor. When that term was up, he did the same thing again. And again, back he came, got his same tractor back, and was happy to be back. I talked to the farm manager and told him, if he put him in the field with a hoe, digging ditches, he would stop doing that. Well, the manager said, "I have a $25,000 tractor sitting there, with no one to drive it. I have hay to mow, silage to gather. This man will drive that machinery from before daylight until 10:00 at night with the headlights on. He would just be a criminal on the street, at least here, he is earning his keep. What do you say you would do?" I say, "I'm glad it's your responsibility, and not mine."

The first year that I was in the office as a clerk, I heard an inmate talking about the dog boy. He was assigned to care for the blood hounds, and any other dogs that happened to be there. When there was an escaped inmate to chase, officers would take the blood hounds and the dog boy to go hunt him down. The dog boy got to believing he was some hot stuff. If the chasing officer happened to be behind when the dog boy caught the escaped inmate, he would beat him up, and tell the officer that the inmate was all bruised because he ran into a swinging limb. He would also challenge every new inmate to a boxing duel. Back in those days, they had boxing gloves furnished to the inmates, and would permit them to box in the recreation center. Anyone that would accept the challenge with the dog boy would wind up getting the stuffing beat out of him. Well, I had an inmate assigned to the business office that had been in the Navy. He was being harassed by the dog boy to get in the ring with him. The dog boy was 190 pounder, and the ex Navy was only 160 pounds. I did not get into any discussions with the inmates about what was going on in the recreation center, but I overheard the discussions in the office between the inmates. Seems that the dog boy was really getting upset because the ex-Navy guy would just ignore his challenges and threats. Finally the ex-Navy man told the dog boy that he was a professional boxer and didn't want to fight any more. That just put gas on the fire for the dog boy. There was just no end to the dog boy's pushing. Finally, a date was set for the match. The coach had to be present when inmates were allowed to box. Well, according to the coach, the smaller man just danced and struck, danced and struck until the dog boy was completely frustrated and worn out. Then he moved in and pulverized him. Word reached the powers to be in Tallahassee, and they stopped all boxing anywhere in the prison system.

Close to the end of the period that we used Bunker C for fuel in our boilers, and switched to electricity and LP gas, a strange thing happened. On the coldest day of the year, which was a Saturday morning, I was called at home by the Security Lieutenant at ACI and told that the fires in neither of the boilers would stay lit, and the steam was all gone. The temperature was only to reach 28 degrees that day. The people in the engineering department said the Bunker C fuel was saturated with water and would not burn. I got dressed and drove to the institution. Just as soon as I got there, I went to the powerhouse. There was plenty of action going on there. The chief engineer had his men draw 29, 55-gallon drums full of water directly out of the tank where a semi-tanker truck had unloaded 10,000 gallons of Bunker C fuel the day before. The 29 barrels was all they had, so they had cranked up the front-end loader and had dug a hole 15 feet in diameter and 10 feet deep, and were draining clear water from a 3" discharge hose into the ground. They had hooked up a propane gas tank to the pilot light to keep it burning as it kept the saturated oil burning trying to keep the dormitories warm enough to keep the inmates from freezing to death. When I saw the situation, I immediately went to my office and called the oil company that sold us the fuel. When I told the official at the oil refinery, he gave me the run around about it being a busted steam line inside of the boiler. I told him we had tested that already, and the exhaust from the pop off valve was clean as a bell.

I asked him if they had a record of the Bunker C that was shipped out the day before. He said, "Of course." I asked, "How much does one storage tank hold?" He said, "160,000 gallons." I asked, "Where was our load shipped from in that tank?" He said,

"The tanker load was number 13 out of that tank." I asked if he had any problem with number 12 or 14. He said, "No." Then I said, "We have pumped 3,500 gallons of clear water out of the tank that was received yesterday." He was beside himself. I said, "We've got to have a good load here today, or someone will pay with their scalp. We have a thousand inmates freezing to death because of this problem." He said, "We will send one of our tankers as soon as we can load it. Is there anything else we can do?" I said, "Yes, but I'll call you Monday with a bill for damages." He said, "Please do that." I went back to the power plant, and stood around until pure Bunker C was coming out of the drain, and then we shut off the drain line. The boilers immediately started to burn better, and about 5 pm we took the gas pilot light off, and it stayed lit.

About 5:30 pm the load of Bunker C showed up, and I talked to the driver. He couldn't add any information, so we let him go after unloading the new fuel. I signed his ticket, and stuck it in my pocket." I said, "It will be a cold day in hell before the state will pay for that load." The driver said, "I don't blame you for that", looking at the mess of drums and hole in the ground. "Well," I said, "I've been working for the state for 26 years, and this is the first time I have ever worked over time. Someone is going to pay for this. Sure enough, the high temperature that day was 28 degrees, and I ruined a good pair of pants and shoes.

All I could think of all weekend long was that mess. Finally I figured out what had happened. The only way that water could get into our tank was to come in with the Bunker C. Then, I got it; when we started using fuel oil instead of coal to heat the boilers, we put three tanks in, a 10,000 gallon tank, and two 20,000 gallon tanks. We had decided the under ground steam tunnels and pipes were beyond repair. In the winter time, you could tell exactly where the steam line ran. The steam was coming up out of the ground all the way from the powerhouse to the dormitories.

The plans were already in place to purchase small boilers for each building that used steam like the kitchen and laundry. The dorms would just use hot water, and two of those heaters were already installed. Then I remembered that I had told the oil company a lie when I said a thousand inmates would freeze to death. There were really only 350 inmates. But, if only one froze to death, they would pay with their scalp, so I didn't even call him and tell him different. Because of these changes, we would, in the near future do away with using Bunker C fuel altogether. We had recently taken the two big bunker tanks out, and were using only the small one.

The previous procedure was this; the trucks would unload the fuel into tank #1 which was the small one. After a 30-minute wait, an inmate would open the valve in the bottom of the tank to drain any of the condensation that might have gathered in the tank, since it was last used. He would let the clear water run out on the ground, and the ground sloped down to a weed bed. The water would either soak in to the ground or evaporate. When the thick oil started to run out, the inmate would shut the valve off, then pump the oil into the bigger tank making room for the next truck load coming in.

I had seen the tankers coming and going, and had asked the drivers if they could reverse the pumps, and load as well as unload the fuel. Their answer was yes. Now, with that information, I wondered just how many times this had happened. My question could not be answered, because the evidence was in the ground. Are you getting the picture yet? The driver saw the inmate draining the water out onto the ground, and he said, "I could unload part of this load at a crooked friend's place, and stop by a stream to finish loading up with clear water. My crooked friend would pay me for half of what he saved. Then, when he unloaded at ACI, the inmate would run the water out on the ground, and no one would be the wiser." But, on this day, the tank that he unloaded into was hooked up directly to the boiler, and just as soon as the water hit, the pilot light went out, and the furnace shut down. The fire went out too. That was the first thing that made us suspicious. Monday morning about coffee break time, I got on the phone, armed with all the evidence and information. I told the oil man that he owed me for 29-55 gallon drums at $5 per drum. He interrupted me and said, "If you will send me an invoice for any damages including overtime for your staff, I will pay." I said, "You are lucky on that point because all of us are on duty 24 hours a day if necessary. So, you won't have any over time to pay." I told him what I had theorized, and told him he had a crooked truck driver. He said, "That Bunker C is hauled for us by a transport corporation that does nothing but haul gasoline and Bunker C, and kerosene for oil companies. I asked him if he knew who was driving on the day in question, and he said, "No." I asked who the transport company was. He said, "I would like for you to let me reimburse you for your trouble. I'm going to give you a credit memo for that load. Any fuel you got out of that load will be free, and any other expense you feel is fair, and let us handle this." I said, "I hate to let you handle it, for I want to see this driver pay for this thing." He assured me he would pay. That is the last I have even thought about this until recently when all of those thieving, conniving CO's were found in those large companies. The first thing that came to my mind was, what if the guy at the oil company was in cohorts with that driver? The only consolation I have is that my employer, the State of Florida, did not lose a red cent on the deal. In fact, we did get some good fuel out of that truck load.

CHAPTER 10
TROUBLE ON THE HORIZON

On June 10, 1993, I went out at 7:45 am and got in my Ford 4-wheel drive hunting vehicle, and started to work as usual. But, before I arrived at work, it was not a usual day. At the top of River Hill on highway 90, I started down the hill. It was one of those crazy three lane roads. Two lanes going up hill and one going down hill. The sun was behind me reflecting off the windshields and chrome bumper, and headlights of two lanes of bumper to bumper traffic. At that time there were 3,000 employees at the Florida State Hospital, and about half of them lived in Jackson County, and were on their way to work at 8 am. That is no problem, I had been meeting those same people on that same hill since 1958. But, never before in all that time was there a tractor pulling a mowing machine in my half of the road. The tractor was out of the road, but 18 inches of his mowing machine was in my lane. It was black just like the surface of the road, with no reflectors on it. Well, I hit the mower with my right front wheel, and it rolled my top-heavy Ford vehicle. I rolled over once, went around the front of the tractor, over the guard rail, and stopped right side up, looking down the steep embankment below, which was at least 100 feet to the bottom, and to the woods. I had my seat belt on, but I lost my hat and my glasses. There was a city police car at Hardee's just across the street. The young policeman came over to me and opened my door and said, "Don't try to move, just put your arms around my neck, and I'll carry you up the hill." I looked at his 160 pound body, and thought, "Man, you've got to be kidding." But, I didn't argue. I did as he said, and when I put my weight on him, we both started to slide down the hill on the grass which was about knee high. I heard a familiar voice say, "Need some help?" It was my life long friend that I taught in Sunday School when he was 13 years old, about 20 years ago. Now he is a huge man of well over 6 feet tall, and well over 200 pounds. I said, "Yes, pull us both. Just get a hold of his belt and pull us up." He did, and we were just the length of the truck down the hill. I then discovered why I did not go down the embankment. The right rear tire on my blazer had caught on the guard rail, and kept me from going over. By the time I sat down on the post of the guard rail, the ambulance was there. The med. tech. took my blood pressure, and said, "It's 300 over 200. Is that normal for you?" I said, "Well, I don't know, this is a first for me. 'Just wait awhile and take it again. I did not just drive over the rail, I rolled this thing down the road and over the rail." "Oh," he said, "I guess I better take you to the hospital." "No, I don't think so," I said. The only place I was hurt was the top of my head. The seat belt was loose enough that it let the top of my head ping the top of the cab. It broke the skin but no more. I noticed my big friend had left, but being the manager of a branch bank was big stuff, and I imagined he needed to get to work. I saw him two weeks later, and he said, "I'm sorry I had to leave you at the wreck last week, but I looked down into that tall grass we were in, and saw a snake slithering between my feet, and like I said, I had to go!" Well, the traffic cops got there in a heart beat, and took one of the east bound lanes, and made a west bound lane, and got the traffic flowing. The roll broke all the glass out of my blazer. Picture this, a hunting and fishing vehicle with a covered body, inside I had axes, shovels, tool box, tackle box, I also had plastic baskets full of shotgun shells. I also had a 19 piece ratchet set scattered all over the road. A big number of the people knew me, and they stopped their cars and helped me pickup all the trash scattered on the pavement, dirt, and grass.

When I got all the stuff picked up, all the small wrenches and shells were accounted for.

Some policeman asked me if I wanted to notify anyone. I said, "Yes, call my wife at home, and tell her to bring the car and pick me up. I don't think I can drive this thing, seeing my motor mount laying out there on the road." He called the police station on his radio, and told them to call my wife, and have her come to Hardee's. Scared her to death, and when she got there, and saw my blazer hanging over the guard rail by one wheel, she did go batty. I also asked him to call the wrecker and he said, "I've already done that." Well, when he told the wrecker man it was a Ford Blazer, he just brought his small pick-up wrecker. He couldn't move it. He had to go back and get his big semi-wrecker to pull it up over the guard rail. I just knew he was going to destroy the guard rail, and I also know if you tear down a rail, they will charge it to you. I talked to the wrecker man when he got it mounted and ready to leave. I said, "What's the charge?" He said, "It's totaled, I'll take the wreck for the bill if it's OK by you." I said, "I just put a new wench on it, if you will let me have the wench, you can have the rest." He said, "OK". "I'll be out later and look for my glasses. I lost them somewhere," I said. I went out that evening and got my wench and glasses. That is the last time I saw the ole blue and white buggy. The next month I replaced it with an 88 model red and white GMC Jimmy. I raised all manner of cane with the State Road Department for letting a mowing machine be out there at 7:30 am to 8:00 am, and 4:30-5:00 PM. They said the tractor had a warning light on it. I said, "About the size of my fist, and about as much light as a lightning bug." I threatened them with everything, even to never using their stinking old highway again. I think that is what brought about a big change because now, never again will a mower be seen on that hill. The state has paved the ground all the way over to the guard rail, and made a passing lane out of that space. My insurance company called me and asked my side of the story because the man that had the contract to mow the right-of-way said that the repairs to the mower were $1,100. I told them not to pay it. Let them take it to court. They said it would cost five times that much in court costs, and lawyer fees. I said, "Well, if you up my insurance premium, the next due date, I'll get me another company for my insurance."

If you have read this book from the beginning, I know you must be saying, all this stuff could not happen to one person. But, it's all true. If I go to putting hair on a story, I'll tell you it has hair. So far, all stories are true. Now, on with the truth.

Early in my career, date not available, I did not make a diary, nor did I make notes. Just in my mind. Dates are not always that important. We were building a dwelling house on the lake overlooking the Jim Woodruff Dam. There was no road to this location. It was about 2,000 feet from the entrance of the institution, so we decided to build a road out to the site. We had a road grader to start leveling down a small hill, so the road would be pretty level. While digging in a clay bank, they broke a leg bone of a person. They stopped grading immediately, came to the office and reported it. Everyone at once said, "I bet it's Shorty." He was a sailor who came home during the second world war, and was last seen walking toward ACI on the railroad track. He was never found. Old people say anytime a bone is found, "I'll bet it's Shorty." Well, we did the usual thing, and called the geographic section of Florida State University. They came right on over, and with tooth brushes, tooth picks, and tweezers, they dug up the rest of the body and carried it back to the University to analyze what we had found. Well, it wasn't Shorty. It was an Indian woman. There used to be a camp site on top of the hill, and they said she was elderly. They could tell by her teeth which were almost worn to the gums from eating dried corn. She was buried squatting down in a round hole dug in the ground. Well, at least we had something to talk about for a while.

Along this same line in 1965, we were digging the foundation to the administration building, and we had to dig down to solid rock. We had the bulldozers going and bones turned up on a push, and the officer in charge called me to see what to do. They knew I was right in the middle of the Indian woman's episode. I remembered what to do, so I called FSU and told them we had unearthed some bones. Were they interested? They said, "Sure, interested, but not excited or alarmed." "Well," I said, "Don't take all year, we are at a stand still." Sure enough, they came the next day, and got what they needed. They said they would write me a letter in a few days, and sure enough they did. They even sent me a picture. The bones came from a manatee. They sent a picture of a complete manatee skeleton that they got from the Fuller's Earth Plant in Quincy, Florida. That earth is real soft and spongy, easy to dig, and the skeleton was easy and complete when they dug it up. So, they were not interested in ours which was embedded in lime rock.

The date, again is unknown. The date is of no importance. Gulf Power was running an electric line from the East Unit at ACI to the West Unit of ACI. They were in front of the poultry project one morning, when a young man showed up and told the crew that he had been hired by Gulf Power and told to report to this crew. One big burley and rough pole climber told him, "You can't work with us with a pony tail. If you work here, you will cut it, or someone else will cut it for you." The hippie said, "I'll not cut it, and no one else will either." The lineman grabbed him, slammed him to the ground, and jerked out his electrician's knife, and with one quick slice, bobbed the pony of it's tail. They got up from the ground, and the lineman said, "You cannot work in front of all these prisoners with a pony tail, but now you can work." The hippie said, "You will be sorry for this." He jumped in his old trap of a car and sped off west. The crew went on about their job. Within 15 minutes the hippie returned with a Sneads' city policeman. The hippie pointed to the big ugly fellow up the pole and said, "That's him." The policeman said, "Did you cut this man's hair by force?" The lineman said, "Guilty as charged. What is my fine?" The policeman said, "$35 for disturbing the peace, and my breakfast." The lineman reached in his front pocket and pulled out a wad of wet from sweat, crumpled up bills and threw down $35, and said, "I'm paid in full. Now, get that hippie out of my sight before I come down there and give you both a hair cut you won't forget. Cop, don't you know you don't have any jurisdiction on prison property?" The policeman picked up the money and said, "Case closed." Now, I must confess that I do not have any proof of the authenticity. But, an eye witness, our assistant construction supervisor saw it, and passed it on to me. I know it had to be true. No one could make up such a story, and the high voltage linemen that I know who lay their lives on the line every day, working with hot 7,200 volts, would tie the devil's tail in a knot. My baby brother worked as a lineman for the Cincinnati, Ohio Electric Company for 30 plus years, and I know him well. He tied the devil's tail in several knots before he retired.

Telling you the story that our assistant construction supervisor told, leads me to tell you something that he did. I know for a fact it is true, and the evidence stands today, and people are living in them. When the federal government was having Perini, Blythe, and Walch contractors to build Jim Woodruff Dam, they built about ten small wooden houses for the government employees. Then, when the dam was completed, the government employees all left, and the houses were no longer needed. They gave five of them to ACI. The assistant supervisor of construction was given the job of getting them from Georgia to ACI. Rather than trying to bring them by highway across that narrow Victory Bridge which spanned the Apalachicola River, he said, "It's just a half-mile across the lake. We will float them across, and they did. And, until this date, 2004, they are at the West Unit with ACI employees living in them.

Now, all these things I tell in the writing of this book may not be what you expect to be in a book about my 38 years in the chain gang, but this book covers it all. Although, everything written herein is involving prisoners directly, it indirectly affects the operation of the whole institution. I think it all is relevant as it's my life.

Now, speaking, or writing about housing for the staff. I recall one shocking incident that took place with the water supply for the housing area. There are 25 dwelling houses at ACI East Unit. East Unit has a water tower, and the West Unit has a water tower, and the dairy has a water tower. One night, our main painter in the construction department was taking a bath in the tub. After he had almost finished bathing, he saw some funny looking creatures in the bath water. He was frightened beyond belief. H e thought that the creatures had come out of him. His wife was a professional nurse, so he called her into the bathroom to give her opinion as to what the little fellows were, and where they had come from. After much deliberation, she decided they did not come out of him, but out of the water supply. So they went into the kitchen, and drew up a pot of water. Sure enough, there were the funny little creatures. Neither knew what they were. They called the main office the next day, and reported what they had found. The engineering department took a water sample and wanted it taken to the laboratory for testing. And guess who they sent? Yes, me. How did you guess? Every time something crazy came up, they would call Gilley. And, that is how I wanted it. I took the two little bottles, and looked at them. I saw the little creatures, and recognized them at once. I used to drink them all the time when I lived on a farm in Kentucky. They were called wiggle tails. I went into the lab, and said to all those snobs in white smocks that had a bad case of the black butt," I brought you some wiggle tails." I thought I was being funny. No one even grinned, and one of them looked down his nose at me and said, "Those are mosquito larvae." I said, "I know that sour puss, all I want from you is to say whether the water is fit for human consumption, and I want it in writing by tomorrow, or I'm coming back over here and wiggle your tails." When I went out the door, I said, "Keep smiling." The people who work in that lab in Tallahassee think they are God's chosen people, and when I go over there and speak to everyone I meet, they stop in their tracks and examine me from head to toe, to see if there is anything that looks familiar to them. Sometimes I stop too, turn, and say at the top of my voice, "Boo!" They really turn their noses up then, and hurry away with a bad taste in their mouths. That never stopped me from speaking to them. Well, enough rabbit chasing.

Back to my important story, you talk about the story traveling like wild fire, everyone knew about the water. The people who lived in the housing area we called the big shots, and some guards also lived there for emergency chases. They were all very concerned about the water safety. Those of us who lived away from the institution in our own homes, and paid for our own water, cut our own grass, and did the maintenance of our own homes, (which they did not), tittered at the wiggle tails. Some of those guys who had been born with a silver spoon in their mouths, and never did get a drink out of a cow track full of wiggle tails, were really upset with the problem, especially the classification supervisor. He complained to high heaven, and even boiled his water. Well, enough said. You get the picture I'm sure. The next day, we received a teletype that said that it was fit for human consumption. The next day, I went to the restroom that was out on the courtyard. I had not gone out doors to go to the toilet since I left the mountains. There I go, chasing rabbits again. You'll have to be patient with me. This is only the second book I have ever written. Anyway, when I went out to the courtyard, you will never guess what I found on the walkway. I found a huge 2" long buffalo bug, with a horn, and pincers, big enough to cut a finger off. Idea....Light bulb!!! I picked him up very carefully, went into the bathroom, got one of those little paper cups out of the dispenser, put just a small amount of water in it, and wrote on the side of the cup "ACI water sample". With bug in cup and water, I took my great project and set it right in the center of the classification supervisor's desk, with no one around. When he came in and saw it, he yelled, "What blankety blank put this on my desk?" When his secretary thought it a bit funny, of course she lived off the grounds, he threatened her with her life! I don't know if he showed it to the big boss or not, but I know if he did, the big boss didn't laugh either. I never did admit to having done that dirty trick, so if that man reads this, he may come looking for me because he still lives here in town, just one street over.

Before I run out of ink, let me tell you how we solved this problem, I knew it had to be in the water tower because the water was pumped directly into the tank from the well. With a pair of binoculars, we could examine the screen wire at the top of the tank where air was let in to keep from creating a vacuum. The screen had rusted away, and there was just pieces left there. All we had to do was replace the screen wire around the top of the water tower, to keep the mosquitoes out, and no more wiggle tails (mosquito larvae).

Sometime in the early 70's we received a federal grant for the MDTA program (Manpower Development Training Act), for the purpose of procuring a bulldozer for training inmates in the art of maintaining, repairing, and operating the machinery. The MDTA director and his instructor of heavy equipment came to see me. They had a problem. The instructor of many years' experience was limited to Caterpillars brand. He said he would be lost with John Deer, Massey- Ferguson, or any other bulldozer. They wanted me to "sole source" the purchase. I said they would never agree to a "sole source". But, if you keep quiet, I'll see what I can do. The central office wanted to personally supervise the bidding process. This was the only time they ever did this to me. But, they let me write the specifications, and I made it clear that the specifications had to be met, no substitution would be acceptable. I took the Caterpillar specification sheet, and copied it word for word. The bid went out, and I requested to be at the bid opening. The purchasing director of Department of Corrections was, and still is, a good friend, and he said, "You've got to be here."

When the bids were opened, International Harvester was low by a few dollars. When we began to check the bid against specifications, the International people were present, as well as Caterpillar and Massey-Ferguson people. My heart jumped when we came to the blade size. International had changed blade length from 10' to 91/2' long. I told the director I wanted International to be removed because of violation of bid condition which said that no substitutions would be accepted. The International man asked, "What difference will 6" make?" I said, "The difference will mean that you won't sell your bull dozer." He said, "I'll weld six inches to the blade. I still don't see why the six inches would matter. Why?" "Because I said, it's what I want," I said, "Are you questioning my ability to know what I want?" He said, "I'll protest it." I said, "May I suggest, before you protest, that you reread the bid specifications that no substitutions will be accepted, and I have your signature on the bid saying that you, by signing, have agreed with the specification." He said, "I still believe that I will protest." I said, "Have you ever heard of black listing nation wide? This is only one sale. Now that you have managed to get on my fighting side, I'll withhold awarding any bid, and use the money for something else. So, I'm sorry. Maybe next time, I'll want your machine. I'd rather you file a protest, than Mr. Caterpillar protest because we violated the conditions of the bid. Your protest will be a lot easier than his would." The man from International had another man with him. I don't think he ever introduced him to us. He leaned over and whispered something to the owner, and he paused for a minute, then he said, "Mr., I have to say, you are a real fighter." I said, "Thanks if you mean it as a compliment. So are you. May I tell my friends back at ACI that we departed friends?" "Of course", he said. He departed, and we awarded the bid to Caterpillar.

CHAPTER 11
BELIEVE IT OR NOT

We imported an assistant farm manager during the 1960s. He was a nervous wreck. He shook so violently that he could not drink coffee unless he held the cup with both hands. I asked someone how he was going to qualify on the pistol range. "Heck, man," he said, "He is one of the best shots that we have." I asked, "How do you figure that?" The answer was, "He should hit the bulls eye, he aims all over the target." Someone that was an eye witness said, "He turns his back to the target, bends over and spreads his legs, braces his elbows on his legs just above his knees. Then he grips the pistol with both hands, aims the pistol upside down, puts the sights on the bulls eye, pulls the trigger, and comes very close to the spot he aims at. If you have a will, you can find a way."

Each year, the last Saturday in October, the employees who worked at ACI before 1968 get together to celebrate the fact that we are still alive. The last meeting, there were only 19 employees still able to make it. I told them I was writing this book, and every last one said they wanted a copy of it.

The youngest man that was ever assigned and sentenced to ACI was 14 years old. He and his older brother and two other boys were caught playing Dr. with a local girl who was 10 years old. The girl's father pressed charges, and the judge said he knew the exact spot to put the two brothers. He was talking about ACI. The brothers were sentenced for 6 months to life. While here for 8 years, they both worked in the construction department. They were paroled out, and we didn't hear from them for 15 years. One day, I was sitting, watching the maintenance and construction manager with three of his buddies who were playing dominoes during lunch hour at the recreation room. A 35-40 year old man entered the room, and came over where we were sitting and asked the construction manager if he was Mr. Melzer. George told him he was. The man held out his hand, and said, "I'm Eddie Bell, and I want to thank you for what you taught me while I was here." He looked at me and said, "I remember you were in the business office, but I can't remember your name." I said, "I'm Mr. Gilley. I remember you. What are you doing now?" He gave me a business card showing Bell Construction Company. I asked about his brother and he said, "He wouldn't gamble to form his own company like I did, but works as a laborer for another man, and is still in Panama City." I asked him what he was doing here. He said, "I married a girl whose parents live in North Carolina, and decided to travel from California where my company is located, and remembered ACI was on Highway 90, and wanted to come by ACI and checkout the place where I got my start." We were all delighted to see him. All five of us remembered him. He was such a tiny little fellow. Everyone noticed him.

I just remembered something funny that I just had to include in the final pages of this book. One day, while doing the inventory on the Industrial Trust Fund Equipment, I was visiting the dairy. They had many 2000 pound Holstein cows. I was out around the silos and noticed some of those monstrous cows, and they were acting crazy. They were staggering, stumbling, and acting silly, shaking their heads and making low moos. I saw a dairy worker, and asked him, "What's wrong with all those milk cows?" He looked out that way and said, "Oh, my goodness, they got into the corn liquor. We have grain corn in the silos, and it has fermented and drained out around the bottom of the silos. And, those darn cows love it and how it makes them feel." He started out toward the cows to drive them into another field, and shut the gate to keep them away from the silos. I asked what effect would it have on the cows. He replied, "Make their milk taste awful."

I'm sure there was a lot of stuff that I missed in my 38 years in the chain gang, but I have no regrets. I think I've had my share. Well, all good things must come to an end. I liked my job, being able to furnish the whole institution with everything from toothpicks to bull bulldozers. But, the last year, I realized it was time for me to go home. I would catch myself getting angry when the phone would ring. I told my secretary, "They are paying me good to answer this phone, and I find myself not wanting to hear someone's problems. It's time for me to retire." She asked, "What do you want for your retirement party?"

A good friend of mine went into the boss's office one day, and put his keys on his desk and said, "I won't be back tomorrow, or ever more. I'm retiring as of right now. I said, "Not that for me. I want all I can get. An orchestra, a band, a quartet, a bunch of cheer leaders, a girl jumping out of a cake, lots of food, lots of gifts, lots of hugs, lots of handshakes, and lots of speeches. I want a return of all I have done for all those who went on before me. I want everything taped on videos, still pictures, the works. Bring in vendors, bosses from regional office, state offices, and I want it all.

Well, I was well pleased. One of the employee's wives suprvised the decorations and delicious refreshments which were all kinds of beautiful fruit, dips and chips, cakes and cookies and drinks. We had the party inside the compound in the staff dining room. One of the first gifts that I opened was a filet knife. My daughter and her husband were taking movie pictures, and the business manager told him, "Get that knife out of here. They are not allowed inside the compound." Next was a hunting knife. They told my son in law to take it to my car. The next gift was a pocket knife. They sent him out the third time. The speakers were the superintendent and others, and they all had a lot of nice things to say. My boss in Tallahassee came and made a good funny speech, and gave me back my half of a commode seat and cover.

The employees collected money and gave me a beautifully engraved watch. They had enough money left over to get me a battery operated screw driver. I thanked them and said, "It will come in handy for I plan to do a lot of screwing while retired." After all the gifts were opened, and all the speeches given, the business manager who was in charge of the party, asked if anyone else had anything to say. Some man stood up in the back of the crowd, and said, "Yes, I do." He was in a black suit, and I couldn't see well enough to tell who it was. As he walked toward the speaker's stand, I realized it was my kid brother from Ohio. I grabbed him and gave him a bear hug. No one knew who he was, and I could see the expression on the faces of those standing close to me. I said, "Oh boy, I've got them now." So, I hugged him again. Then, I turned to them and said, "This is my little brother from Cincinnati. I didn't know he was coming." He made a speech about me being the brother with all the looks, and the money and friends, but not as much brains as he, because he had been retired for two years already. When the crowd found out who my brother was, they clapped and yelled really loudly. They didn't know how to act because Gilley didn't just hug other men.

That day was Oct. 31,1995. I turned 65 years old in two days. That was not the happiest day in my life. It was less than my marriage, my daughter's birth, my granddaughter's birth, but it does rank above my dates of three open heart surgeries, and my truck wreck. Well, you know what I felt.

That was 8 years ago, and I have only been back to ACI two times to retirement parties. I feel about the time I pulled at ACI like the time I pulled in Uncle Sam's army. I wouldn't take anything for the experiences I had, but I wouldn't give you a nickel for any more.

ABOUT THE AUTHOR

Mr. Gilley was born in Grays, Kentucky on November 2, 1930, to Fred and Lora Gilley, the fourth of six children. His family moved to Lynch, Kentucky sometime between his birth and age 5. He attended the Lynch Independent Elementary School and High School owned and operated by US Steel Company where he lettered in football. Here he went to school with Wilma Lewis, and in 1951, on May 5th, they were married. Nine months later he was drafted into the Army, and then volunteered for the Paratroopers. He was stationed at Fort Bragg, and they lived in Fayetteville, North Carolina nearby.

www.ingramcontent.com/pod-product-compliance
Lightning Source LLC
Chambersburg PA
CBHW051422280526
45785CB00003B/1120